Quite the accomplishment.

— Dr. Jordan B. Peterson
CLINICAL PSYCHOLOGIST AND BEST SELLING AUTHOR

Read this book if you want to be challenged on what an abundant life in Christ means. Read this book if you're tired of the false presupposition of performance theology. Thomas is a friend who helped me freshly unpack the story of the prodigal son. This frank reflection of life in the ministry is powerful.

— D. Clay Perkins, Ph.D.
FORMER PRESIDENT OF ROANOKE BIBLE COLLEGE

Out of his own personal pain, Thomas has found the courage to introduce us to a fresh understanding of the prodigal son and his family (Luke 15). Not only does he tell the story with imaginative clarity; he also presents the Biblical lessons and concepts in a very understandable form. The reader will appreciate the personal applications of the parable.

– Marvin L. Garrison
EXECUTIVE DIRECTOR OF HI-PLAINS SCHOOL OF MISSIONS

Highly recommend this book. When you read it, be sure to have a highlighter handy, as you are going to want to mark many pages to re-read and focus on again.

— Sandy Peplin
AVID READER

A must-read for anyone who is depressed by circumstances, challenged in their faith that God cares, and about to cop-out. It's for those who often get burnt out trying to live up to everybody's expectations. Based on The Prodigal Son (a parable), the book reveals how the dilemma of both sons presents us with the age-old problem of seeing our value in our doing. All I can say is, Kilian's discovery of the answer to our problem and his embodiment of it, this is what I want for myself too.

— Fleur Marie Vaz
CHIEF EDITOR OF MALAYSIAN EDUCATIONAL SERVICES

A must-read book. It helps you understand yourself better. If you believe in God or not, this book is an excellent guide to opening yourself to the new and the correct. Entertaining read, so much so that I couldn't put it down until I read the complete book.

— Dina Husseini
DEVELOPMENTAL EDITOR AND AUTHOR AT PEN IT! PUBLICATIONS, LLC

Kilian challenges the status quo of a performance-based culture that we've all accepted since birth. His writing style engages your heart and mind in a personable fashion. A must-read for everyone considering or are participating in pastoral ministry. There is nothing like this book; you will not be disappointed by it.

— Austin Keller
SENIOR PASTOR, UBLY CHRISTIAN CHURCH

Enjoyed this book and the encouragement the author gives for people stuck in a performance mindset. I am one of those people that value doing much more than being. I appreciated the sharing of the personal struggles that the author has gone through to help illustrate the concepts. Written very well and easy to read, I highly recommend this book.

— Phil Parker

CAMPUS MINISTER AT VIRGINIA TECH UNIVERSITY, AND FOUNDER OF VICTORY 44 INTERNATIONAL REFUGEE AND CAMPUS MINISTRY

The book is old knowledge in a new perspective. The astonishing facts brought to light and the format piques the interest. Kilian's journal entries throughout are inspirational and compelling. There are many excellent principles within, and the allegories used resonated with me. *Start Being, Stop Doing* gets my recommendation!

— Jennifer Rivera

AUTHOR OF *THE BARN* AND *THE JOURNEY HOME*

Start Being, Stop Doing

Transforming our sense of self by ending our obsession with performance.

Thomas A. Kilian III

CHATHAM, VIRGINIA

2022

The content, views, and opinions expressed in this book are those of the author and do not necessarily reflect the position of any of the contributors, entities, and non-entities mentioned. References are not to be read unfailingly as endorsements. The author has made every effort to provide accurate internet addresses at the time of publication.

Start Being, Stop Doing. Copyright © 2021 by Thomas A. Kilian III

All rights reserved. No part of this publication may be reproduced, stored in or introduced into a retrieval system, or transmitted in any form, or by any means, without prior written permission of the publisher, except for uses as provided by United States of America copyright law.

To request permissions, contact the publisher at permissions@hybridpublishing.press.

Hardcover: 978-1-7374475-3-5

Paperback: 978-1-7374475-0-4

Ebook: 978-1-7374475-1-1

Library of Congress Control Number: 2021914038

Hardback Edition, August 2022

Cover Image: A derivative of "Pierre Puvis de Chavannes The Prodigal Son c. 1879," by National Gallery of Art used under CC0 BY 1.0.

Unless otherwise indicated, Scripture quotations are from the ESV® Bible (The Holy Bible, English Standard Version®), copyright © 2001 by Crossway, a publishing ministry of Good News Publishers. Used by permission. All rights reserved.

Scripture quotations marked NASB are from the (NASB®) New American Standard Bible®, Copyright © 1960, 1971, 1977, 1995, 2020 by The Lockman Foundation. Used by permission. All rights reserved. www.lockman.org

Scripture quotations marked NIV are from the Holy Bible, New International Version®, NIV® Copyright © 1973, 1978, 1984, 2011 by Biblica, Inc.® Used by permission. All rights reserved worldwide.

All emphases in Scripture quotations have been added by the author.

Printed in the United States of America under the imprint of Hybrid Publishing, a division of Kilian Enterprises LLC • U.S.A VACC ID 11138834

Dedication

To my parents, Tom and Sandie,

and my sister Helen

who gave me a home

when I had none.

Besides being wise, the Preacher also taught the people knowledge, weighing and studying and arranging many proverbs with great care. The Preacher sought to find words of delight, and uprightly he wrote words of truth. The words of the wise are like goads, and like nails firmly fixed are the collected sayings; they are given by one Shepherd. My son, beware of anything beyond these. Of making many books there is no end, and much study is a weariness of the flesh. The end of the matter; all has been heard. Fear God and keep his commandments, for this is the whole duty of man. For God will bring every deed into judgment, with every secret thing, whether good or evil.

— **Ecclesiastes 12:9-14**

Contents

Introduction:		My Encounter With Death Almost Killed Me • *1*
Ch.	1	Why We Do: Nakedness And Fig Leaves • *6*
	2	In The Eye Of the Beholder: Who Are You? • *16*
	3	He Wanted Dad Dead • *22*
	4	God Is Dead? • *28*
	5	The "Indecent" Luxury Of Rejection • *36*
	6	The Law Of Addiction • *46*
	7	Purgatory: An Affair With Do • *66*
	8	Change Of Heart • *82*
	9	Limping Home • *88*
	10	Merit Is Overrated • *100*
	11	Grace Is Always Greater • *112*

12	Getting Over Yourself • *118*
13	Life At Home • *136*
14	Tailor-Made • *146*
15	The Art Of Celebration • *156*
16	Doers Are Party Poopers • *170*
17	The Initiative Is With Who? • *178*
18	To Be Or Not To Be • *190*
19	The Ordinary Christian Life • *212*
20	Made Alive • *222*
21	Engaging The Monotony w/ Celebration • *236*
22	If There's Anything To Do, Then Sit • *250*

Conclusion:
With Is Greater Than Do • *265*

Word From The Author • *273*

Introduction: My Encounter With Death Almost Killed Me

"I'm guilty of not being perfect." I penned these words with the strength given to me by several hours of sleep induced by sedatives. Medications kept me alive during my hospital stay. I arrived there wearing dark dress pants and a solid-colored button-up shirt only halfway buttoned. I could have been mistaken for a social worker if only I still had my shined shoes. They took them away because their laces would help put me out of misery.

Just several hours before admission to the mental ward, I held a knife to my throat, determined to leave the world behind. Failing at suicide, I spent three days of my extended life under evaluation.

Reluctantly, I sat through cheesy group therapy sessions. Patients were instructed to paint with "think positive" stencils or write what you valued about yourself. The latter, I didn't do well in. Patients discussed problems as if they were petty habits. Within the group setting, everyone protested they didn't belong in a mental ward. They were all misunderstood as having a problem. Rationalizing why this was, I thought, *Who wants to have a problem, anyway?* One-on-one conversations revealed, however, that each felt something was very wrong with them.

Several had serious mental disorders, like a schizophrenic guy named Paul. He had to sleep in the hallway to "keep away from the demons that dragged him into hell." He had forced his way into my room to share how voices inside his head told him how "God hated him," so he ran down a highway naked in shock of "his eternal rejection." He continued to state how he was "now in purgatory." He had interrupted himself to ask, "Why are you here... in purgatory?" I didn't know whether to laugh or cry.

I was ashamed. I thought, *Should I try to counsel him instead of answering?* My silence increased Paul's irritability. "So, I tried to kill myself. I'm dressed this way because I was to officiate a funeral today."

Paul yelled, "Wait! You're a minister, and you did that? Wow, bro. A minister here in purgatory!"

Holding back from correcting his bad doctrine with my years of biblical and theological training, I replied, "Well, I am here with you."

Although unbiblical, experiencing "purgatory" isn't entirely myth. In some weird way, Paul was right. I was inhabiting a place of suffering and a different plane of existence. Didn't know how I got there. But it sure felt familiar, like I belonged. Maybe it was because I was treating life as a kind of purgatory—a place of trying to atone for the wrongness I felt. I was caught in an in-between place, where I could choose life or death.

I spent several days in the hospital trying to figure out how I'd slipped into despair so badly convinced that I was the problem and the solution was getting rid of me. The only truth before me were my feelings—anxiety, anger, despair, confusion, and fear. My feelings instructed me that in death, my tormented soul could find rest. After my encounter with death, I learned that my suicide attempt was the unfortunate response to the death I felt in a series of traumatic encounters when shamed with, "There's something wrong with you, Thomas."

After my release from hospital, I was forced to resign from my role as a minister at a church. I lost my home and much of my community's support. I felt like a walking dead man. "I am unfit to live but not ready to die," I would mumble. Being unhappy was normal. Life felt absent of meaning as death seemed to linger over me. I thought I knew why I was miserable and depressed. It was because my fiancée rejected me. It was because I lost my job, home, and friends. It was because I was fat. But as life "normalized," the unhappiness still lingered and the past seemed just as threatening, maybe even more so. Life was without dignity, significance, or direction—but why?

One day I became increasingly aware that I felt like the bad guy in everything. I was terrible at relationships. A bad boyfriend. An imperfect minister. Heck, I was even worse at being a human. It wasn't that I felt bad because I was evil as much as feeling guilty for not being perfect. My dignity was wrapped up in what I did—how I performed in relationships, work, and in daily tasks. When I didn't perform well, I lost dignity and all hope of acceptance.

"Your problem is perfectionism. Just stop it! All is right," people would share.

Not only was the advice unhelpful, but it was untrue—all was not right—and it brought me more frustration. As much as I read about "overcoming" and "winning," nothing helped. Increased knowledge only aggravated my dissatisfaction with life because I became more and more aware of how imperfect I was.

My transformation finally came after realizing the desire for perfection or the fear of imperfection was not my problem. The problem—as with so many others I encounter—is the horror of knowing I am flawed and broken. The truth is, we've never thrived in a world where acceptance is dependent on performance. Just check out the stories of well respected people (although initially considered odd) who thrived and changed the world. They talk about how unconditional acceptance in relationships created life within and spurred them on—not demands. But our Western culture demands flawless performance to get anywhere in life—status and wellbeing in life come from it. Even within "Shame and Honor" cultures of the Eastern world, the performance of what's honorable—things on the to-do list—determines one's value or standing in society.

We've attached our value to our performance. No wonder people struggle with their imperfections! There's no way to get around the world's demands—unless there is a new way to life utterly separate from work-based acceptability.

This has led me to write this book. It is for anyone who is depressed by circumstances, challenged in their faith that God cares, about to cop out, or looking for an alternative to religion. The book details how our sense of self can be transformed, finding wellbeing—absolute value and meaning—by ending our obsession with performance. The book is all about *being* rather than *doing* to please God and to be established in our identity as sons and daughters of

God. It does this by threading some key principles through Jesus' story of *The Prodigal Son* in Luke 15. Three perspectives—the prodigal son, the elder brother and the father—are explored to show different expectations, visions and responses to "home"—the state of well-being.

The Luke 15 verses are explored in sections through the narrative and are reinforced with biblical accounts to deepen the study. All of which demonstrate how an open, broken, humble and contrite spirit is the ground for greater intimacy and revelation—but a haughty spirit God will reject.

The substantive development of the narrative is based on my own insights which have arisen from painful, even traumatic experiences with people, and led to two failed suicide attempts. Although the accounts of the people who rejected and scoffed at me are demeaning and brought me to great lows, revelation through the Word, and a personal encounter with the Father and the risen Christ took me to a whole new level of relationship—a whole new plane of existence.

This is what I want for you too.

By the end of this book, it's my hope that the truth that being is greater than doing is made the core reality of our soul, so we would stand utterly transformed and indistinguishable from our source, set aglow, and forever freed.

1 Why We Do:
Nakedness and Fig Leaves

Figure 1: *Hiding Our Nakedness*

So when the woman saw that the tree was good for food, and that it was a delight to the eyes, and that the tree was to be desired to make one wise, she took of its fruit and ate, and she also gave some to her husband who was with her, and he ate. Then the eyes of both were opened, and they knew that they were naked. And they sewed fig leaves together and made themselves loincloths.

And they heard the sound of the Lord God walking in the garden in the cool of the day, and the man and his wife hid themselves.

— **Genesis 3:6-8a**

Do you try to hide your true self from others—faults and things you believe are the unacceptable parts of you? My guess is yes. Biblically, it's the same reaction of Adam and Eve, the first humans, in the discovery of their nakedness (see Genesis 3). I always imagined Adam as perfectly sculpted and Eve most appealing. Being the first humans meant they were perfect, right? So why hide your nakedness? The forbidden fruit they ate opened their eyes to their nakedness—not that they weren't naked before, but their perception of nudity changed. Nakedness, with its vulnerability, was something to fear and something to hide. In their moment of imperfection, their bodies instantly became the image of "defect"—or at least in their perception—and not the image of God they once knew. Something was wrong with them. In shame, they covered their nakedness with fig leaves.

Like Adam and Eve, as much as we like to hide it, we know that something is wrong with us. I believe that you know that something is wrong, and you're trying to clean yourself—hide, prove yourself, earn your keep. Because of it, you and I, along with humanity, are obsessed with "do." The fig leaves we wear are evidence. Think of your college degree as a giant fig leaf. Similarly, your relationships, talents, knowledge, and net worth. To wear a fig leaf is what humanity does best—parade and cover—but in each culture differently.

Humanity is ever trying to answer the big questions of life, which everyone must have working answers for to live. Such questions range from "Who are we as human beings? What's wrong with us?" to "Is there anything that would help us improve ourselves? What would put us right?" Most of us have working ideas or philosophies about these big questions. Most address "What's wrong with us and how we can right ourselves?" Perhaps this is why self-help sections in bookstores are so large. Though every person tends to be overly optimistic about how original their working ideas are, let me put it to you that there are four to six significant systems of thought which have highly influenced our ideas of how to live.[1] (And that thought I wrote isn't my original either. Check out the footnote.)

Interestingly, the existence of thought systems reveals where we suspect we've gone wrong and need fixing, in short, that we're naked. There's a "Dos" and "Don'ts" system to cover oneself from nakedness in every major religion. And just as God said to Adam and Eve, "Who told you that you were naked?" I would suggest we ask ourselves a similar question: "Who told you that you had to cover up your nakedness?"

In our awareness of imperfections and hang-ups, the world has "Do" systems of belief which alert us: "We must do everything at whatever the costs to fix ourselves." The truth is we have made ourselves naked, so please don't feel alone in feeling broken, damaged, imperfect, and anxious to hide or fix it. We're all in the same boat. But, gladly, there's an alternative way of living to the cover-up system.

Unlike religions, Christianity isn't concerned with rituals and rites for us to be made right. The background belief in Christianity is that one can't do anything to achieve perfection and approval.

In the first century, during the spread of Christianity from the Eastern Mediterranean throughout the Roman Empire, Apostle Paul writes to churches how people of Jewish heritage—whose culture was a product of Judaism—were converting to Christianity. They converted with the radical belief that "a person is not justified by works of the law but through faith in Jesus Christ" (Galatians 2:16). Those who followed them "believed in Christ Jesus, in order to be justified by faith in Christ and not by works of the law, because by works of the law no one will be justified" (Galatians 2:16). By following the law system (dos and don'ts), people saw how no one was perfected under the law. Paul made it a point to the churches in Rome that, although the law was good and necessary to keep justice and goodness, he found that adherence to religious rules in his early life created an inward struggle:

> *I was once alive apart from the law, but when the commandment came, sin sprang to life, and I died. I found that the very commandment that was intended to bring life actually brought death... For sin, seizing the*

opportunity afforded by the commandment, deceived me, and through the commandment put me to death. So then, the law is holy, and the commandment is holy, righteous and good. Did that which is good, then, become death to me? By no means! Nevertheless, in order that sin might be recognized as sin, it used what is good to bring about my death, so that through the commandment sin might become utterly sinful... We know that the law is spiritual; but I am unspiritual, sold as a slave to sin... I do not [approve of] what I do. For what I want to do I do not do, but what I hate I do. And if I do what I do not want to do, I agree that the law is good. As it is, it's no longer I myself who do it, but it is sin living in me. For I know that good itself does not dwell in me, that is, in my sinful nature. For I have the desire to do what is good, but I cannot carry it out. For I do not do the good I want to do, but the evil I do not want to do—this I keep on doing... Although I want to do good, evil is right there with me... What a wretched man I am! Who will rescue me from this body that is subject to death? Thanks be to God, who delivers me through Jesus Christ our Lord! (Romans 7:9-19; 21, 24-25 NIV)

Do you empathize with Paul's struggle? Paul is talking about his battle with the religious law that was familiar to Jews. But we can also think of law in a general sense. Law could be anything you feel you ought to do. Because here is what I know about you. (And please don't be offended because I don't know you.) What you think you ought to do, you don't do consistently. It may not be the Ten Commandments, the Bible, or rules within a religion. But you internally have something that says, *This is what I need to do*. But you don't do it. There's "Here's what I ought to do. I would be better off doing this. I would be healthier, a better spouse or parent, a better person."

Then there is another part of you that does what you should not do. Now, adults have an idea of what that is. "I don't do what I know I should do—that which I'm convicted to do. I don't even do what's good for me," we say in disgust, repulsed by ourselves. If internal rules and God's natural laws, which are already evident in the world, create contempt for the imperfect, then external laws will only add to that.

And the "ought-tos" are endless. There're subsets of culture, each with its codes of conduct—a further list of dos and don'ts. Thus, there are many systems of law in which you and I become exposed for who we are—imperfect and unacceptable. In every religious community, there's a strict system of dos and don'ts to be made right and strong disapproval for those who don't adhere. It's the apparent response from those who believe that God withholds any goodness from the offender. And it adds to the heap of shame—disgust felt by you or by others about you—for not behaving by the rules.

Like disgust, we discuss shame with ambiguity. As Edward T. Welch, Ph.D., comments, "It's hard to know how to speak about the unspeakable."[2] Although you may not have realized it, you already experience hints of shame when you're embarrassed.

Welch continues, "You pick your nose in public and get caught. You break out in acne, and someone points it out. At those moments, you don't fit in, and everyone knows it. There is a momentary rupture of relationships. You turn red. You wish you could die, right on the spot."[3] Although embarrassment has hints of shame, when talking about real shame, we are not talking about the inconvenient moment of humiliation—that can be slowly but surely brushed away like dandruff. Shame doesn't dissolve with time, nor can it be laughed at like embarrassment. The difference between shame and embarrassment is how shame grips our soul's core and becomes our identity.

The moment I identified shame and saw its bloody fangs, I was fortunate to have escaped alive. It came when someone promised to love me and not only didn't but refused to love me at all. It was also a room full of men telling me I was "unfit" for work. And for shame to wear off, it felt that my very body had to wear away. Soon, I was confessing things as my fault when they weren't. It was my fault for being the target of someone's anger. It was my fault for being hurt and rejected by people I had loved—I deserved it! I was at fault for being alive and even being born. If you have ever been that forsaken person, you know far too well how easy it is to take all the blame.

The realization that something is wrong with us comes to us in different ways at different times. A gentleman once told me his parents sat him down before leaving him to start his life. They told him, "You'll never amount to anything. You're nothing." I once heard a lady say to a preacher, "I felt comfortable hugging my dead dog, but I could never bring myself to touch a dead relative. Is there something wrong with me? What's wrong with me?" The lady is not alone in her question. Everyone can be heard in all their activities and religions, saying, "I feel so wrong, but don't know why… maybe this is why…"

The shame that hounds us is elusive and appears to be the general human condition. Shame doesn't want to be exposed. It often hides in the shadow of guilt. Shame is where even forgiveness brings no relief, nor does a guilty verdict make atonement. Shame moves into our lives in several ways: 1) By what happened to us. 2) By the result of our associations. 3) By what we have or haven't done or are currently doing.[4] Shame seems to be in the fabric of humanity living in a broken world: one need not look long to find shame's thread within us all.

If we only paused in the busyness that we hid within and gazed into our lack of contentment, we'd find shame and its cause. For many women, it's easier to identify shame—"It's there, and I know it." For many men, we don't necessarily know that shame is there, but we may feel it—"I feel the little boy within me when _____ happens."[5] All it takes is one action or word from the right person. And all it takes is nothing—no interest or embrace—from the right person.[6]

In his book *Healing for Damaged Emotions*, David Seamands normalizes our experience with shame. He writes:

> *Many Christians... find themselves defeated by the most powerful psychological weapon that Satan uses against Christians... Its name? [Shame.]... a gut-level feeling of inferiority, inadequacy, and low self-worth... This feeling shackles many Christians... Although they understand their position as sons and daughters of God, they are tied up in knots, bound by a terrible feeling of inferiority, and chained to a deep sense of worthlessness.*[7]

In light of shame, do we need anyone to tell us "Stop it"? Do we need diet books? Books that tell you how to save money? People who tell you that this or that will fix your marriage? Maybe not. Do you need somebody to say, "Work harder"? Do we need any more advice? Our problem is not within knowing what to do to solve our problem but within knowing that we're unable to solve it—perpetually imperfect.

So how do we stop doing and start being the person we want to be?

By looking throughout the Christian Bible, we'll discover the liberating answers given by Jesus Christ and His apostle, Paul. We'll first discuss Jesus' answer given in the form of a story—yep, thankfully, Jesus doesn't give advice: He reveals. We'll also discuss His response to shameful moments. Then we'll peer into the life and teachings of Apostle Paul to discover how to win in our struggle against do.

2 In the Eye of the Beholder:
Who Are You?

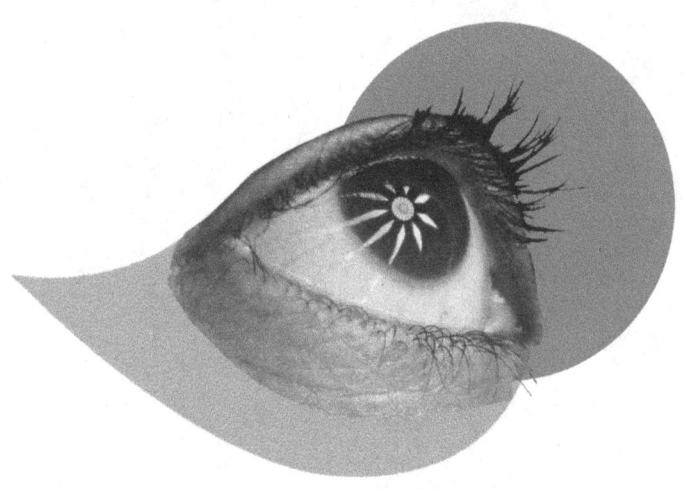

Figure 2: *Beholder*

Within the New Testament, we find Jesus in-between two groups: the law-keepers and the law-breakers, the behaving and the misbehaving. On the one hand, we have people who felt close to God because they did most things right. And, in contrast, we have those who thought they'd never know where they stood with God because they did most things wrong. Nevertheless, both groups had one thing in common: they believed that God's view of them was based on their performance—what they did or didn't do.

In any religion, these two groups exist. They believe the quality of life in the here-and-now and the hereafter is in measure to their performance. For the most part, no matter your religion, everyone struggles with "What does God think about me?" Those of gnostic and atheistic persuasions can sympathize here because there's value in enlightenment and truth—the absence of ignorance—these can be appreciated because they haven't yet been appropriated and made constants in our lives.

We all experience a deep desire to not only live and gift the world but to leave our mark, in a word: belong. Since we feel that we are somehow wrong, stained, imperfect—don't make the mark— we're driven to prove that we're not bad people—a mistake. Many dedicate entire lifespans to accumulating wealth, affirmation, achievements, and relationships. However, in the second half of their life, many consider their gains to be meaningless. To quote Mike Tyson, considered one of the best heavyweight boxers of all time,

"I've lived for garbage... all of this is nothing."[1]

This brings me to the question: "When you think about God thinking about you, what do you think about?" Bit of a tongue twister, I know, but it's a big idea. I originally heard it in a sermon by Andy Stanley, and I couldn't shake it. As we move throughout our time together, it will become apparent that what you think about when thinking about God thinking about you has a massive impact on what you feel about yourself. It also affects how you think about others and God, in a word—life. When we begin to think about who we are and our worth, we start bouncing thoughts off things that could be far-reaching. It impacts the way that we live. Here are some of those things that influence how we think of God when He's thinking about us.

First of all, the most significant influence when we think about who we are—well—is how we feel about ourselves. We generally believe that the way God thinks about us is close to what we think about us. And that changes from day-to-day. Think about what a good day for you looks like. Maybe it's living morally upright. Perhaps you got up a little earlier to meditate and read. Maybe you were nice to your spouse. Maybe your decision to stop yelling at your kids makes you feel like a competent parent. You let an elderly adult have your seat on a bus or paid for someone's order. Overall, you've had a good day. My point is, isn't it true that when you've had a good day, you think existence is grand or that God is happy with you? Absolutely!

Well, what happens when you have a bad day? You're convinced that God is merciless towards you because the universe is tilted a little more towards chaos. It's when that lousy habit comes back into your life. And now you're feeling like an awful person. Maybe you were disloyal to your partner or friend. It could be that you weren't strictly honest at work. Perhaps you didn't disclose everything on the farm to the taxman. Now there's a cloud of guilt, and it confirms what you most hate about yourself—that's shame. It's a bad day, and you're not happy. And isn't it true that when you're not satisfied with yourself, you assume that God has no compassion for you?

I want to be very frank here and tell you that assuming that God's attitude towards you is a copy of yours is a bizarre way to live. As if God should take His cues from you! Now you may not necessarily believe this, but that's how you often live. The self-hatred and discomfort in yourself serve as evidence of this reality; God becomes just as fickle, moody, unpredictable, and unloving as you are towards yourself.

Secondly, the most significant influence on us when we think about who we are is simply people and culture in general. We learned a long time ago that things wouldn't go well if we didn't perform well. Performance is everything! We had to perform at school. Then we had to perform at work. We needed to perform in the marketplace. Some of us feel like we have to perform in our relationships. How about performing for our parents? Maybe some of us were compared to our dependable older sister or our talented brother. Some of us feel like we must act in our marriages to get the love we need. Some of us may have never experienced "love" that wasn't performance-based. Maybe it was just the way that some of us were raised.

So when we think about who we are, our worth, and what God thinks about us, it's natural for us to think, "Well, it must be in the measure of what my performance is." You may not think of yourself, others, and God precisely in those terms, but in our natural responses, we often do.

What these two influencers have in common—"What I think about me" and "What people and culture think about me"—is how they revolve around one word: do. We tend to think and emotionally operate as if our value is through the lens and the filter of what we do.

What if this measure of our worth is wrong? What if God doesn't take His cues about you from you? What if God operates on a completely different system and sliding scale? What if He's in a different economy of relationships than us humans? What if our identity and value are free of what we do or don't do? If our performance has no bearing on our approval and our ability to have a fulfilled life… then, who are we, and what does life become?

Christ made it His life's mission to tell us what God thinks about us. One of the ways He addressed us on this subject was His message with the title of *The Prodigal Son*. It's one of Jesus' best-known parables. It's a story about a father and two performance-driven sons. One is a son who did most things right because he wanted to be home but never came to know what it was to be home. The other son did everything wrong, even asking his father to die prematurely to receive his inheritance, but who was able to come home and be reconciled with his father.

As we move together, we'll discuss Jesus' parable and His good news from the viewpoints of 1) doers, 2) those who do nothing, and 3) God who does everything. Just as Jesus' message provided His original audiences with answers to their questions, we are provided solutions to our existential questions: "What's life about? What can make my life right?"

3 He Wanted Dad Dead

Figure 3: *Judas Betrays Jesus*

Now the tax collectors and sinners were all drawing near to hear him [Jesus]. And the Pharisees and the scribes grumbled, saying, "This man receives sinners and eats with them"

... And he [Jesus] said, "There was a man who had two sons. And the younger of them said to his father, 'Father, give me the share of property that is coming to me.' And he divided his property between them. Not many days later, the younger son gathered all he had and took a journey into a far country, and there he squandered his property in reckless living."

— Luke 15:1-2; 11-13

When you read the Bible accounts of Jesus' life and ministry, it's incredible to find how wherever He went, the people who were nothing like Him, liked Him. Even stranger, the people who had major issues seemed to be enjoyed by Jesus. Remarkably, the only people who Jesus didn't like were those who taught others that God only liked good people.

Here's what this means for us: If you were approached by Jesus today in the market, He would like you. What do I mean by like? Well, He would want to be with you because He wants the best for you, despite your skin color, background, habits and hang-ups, your weirdness, and your sins. What we're talking about is His compassion for you. Maybe His compassion is more unconditional than we might think.

As mentioned in chapter two, Jesus always has two groups in His audience. In the book of Luke, chapter fifteen, we find Him in-between the law-keepers and the law-breakers: "Now the tax collectors and sinners were all drawing near to hear him [Jesus]. And the Pharisees and the scribes grumbled, saying, 'This man receives sinners and eats with them.'"

Here we have the Pharisees/Scribes and the tax collectors/sinners. The Pharisees (also called "Doctors of the Law") were a significant Jewish sect in Jesus' time devoted to the exact observance of the Jewish religion. They were separatists known as the "righteous."[1] The Scribes mentioned were another organized group, characterized as the wise who dedicated their lives to studying and interpreting the Mosaic Law.[2]

Then we have the tax collectors, who were private government subcontractors of Rome, also known as "publicans." According to Dwayne H. Adams in his book *The Sinner in Luke*, "The [tax-collectors] were in a profession that was open to dishonesty and oppression of their neighbor" as they often over-taxed others to line their own pockets (see Luke 19:8).[3] The folks in the category of "sinner" (as distinct from the "righteous") were seen as enemies of Israel. "Sin" and "sinner" became charged sectarian terms used to condemn and ostracize those violating cultural norms.[4] Essentially, the two groups of Jesus' audience were the doers and the non-doers, the latter being those who sat and listened to Jesus. Not surprisingly, the two groups didn't like each other.

As doers often do, the Pharisees and the scribes are grumbling here. They complain, "How can Jesus, a godly teacher, have anything to do with non-doers? Not only that, but how could he befriend them and have a good time at their dinner parties—what's there to celebrate, anyway? He never sat with us although we've been doing the Lord's work!"

What's interesting here is what the sinners are doing in contrast to the religious. They're "drawing near" to be with Jesus so they can hear Him. While sinners are with Jesus, the doers do their thing—complaining and critiquing people's performance. The doers don't understand Jesus being with the non-doers. As far as they know, God and godly people are concerned about doing the right things. Their frustration is a cause of conflict.

As the conflict between the doers and the non-doers reaches boiling point in Luke fifteen, Jesus, as we will soon see, talks to them in a way that brings them on the same page. Although different, both groups believe their value was measured by what they did or didn't do. The religious folks felt close to God because they did many good things but were obsessively doing it in fear of disapproval. In contrast, the sinners thought they would never know where they stood with God because they mainly did wrong things. To be sure, the question both groups have is, "What must we do to achieve acceptance?" It's our question too.

Jesus knew their desire for acceptance in an intimate sense of belonging. So Jesus, to address their heart condition, crafts a gut-wrenching story to say, "You have it wrong. The way you're valued is not how you, people, or even the culture values you." Here's the first part of His story:

> *And he [Jesus] said, "There was a man who had two sons. And the younger of them said to his father,*

> 'Father, give me the share of property that is coming to me.' And he divided his property between them. Not many days later, the younger son gathered all he had and took a journey into a far country, and there he squandered his property in reckless living" (Luke 15:11-13).

At first glance, we may struggle to realize what's happening here. Remember, Jesus has two groups in the audience. And He's preparing to tell them why He loves everyone by giving a parable—a made-up story to express a truth. Now, recognize that parables like *The Prodigal Son* aren't designed to make us feel all warm and fuzzy. Parables are generally not requested. There are no parables at poetry readings because parables make your head hurt. As a genre, by design, parables are to challenge and shake up the status quo.

In His parable, Jesus uses a situation that Kenneth E. Bailey discusses as an unheard-of event:

> *I have been asking people of all walks of life from Morocco to India and from Turkey to Sudan about the implications of a son's request for his inheritance while the father is still living. The answer has always been emphatically the same... the conversation runs as follows: Has anyone ever made such a request in your village? Never! Could anyone ever make such a request? Impossible! If anyone ever did, what would happen? His father would beat him, of course! Why? The request means—he wants his father to die... After signing over his possessions to his son, the father still has the right to live off the proceeds... as long as he is alive. Here the*

> *younger son gets, and thus is assumed to have demanded, disposition to which, even more explicitly, he has no right until the death of his father.*[5]

In effect, we have an unheard-of event of a son telling his father, "Listen, Dad. I've been waiting for the day you keel over that I may receive my inheritance in full. So can we pretend that you died?" Now, even the worst tax collector and sinner in Jesus' audience is going, "That's bold! Even though I'm a greedy sinner, I would never think of doing that."

The implication "Father, I cannot wait for you to die" underlies his requests.[6] It couldn't get much worse in a father-son relationship. It's emotional. And Jesus gives an extreme example of repulsive behavior. So now both groups in His audience are on the same page: Here's a rejection of a father by a son, who now deserves to be beaten and forsaken. There's no statement on their agreement in this, but to be sure, their cultural upbringings would have instructed them to vote the son "off of the island."

4 Is God Dead?

Figure 4: *God On The Cross*

> *I said in my heart, "Come now, I will test you with pleasure; enjoy yourself." But behold, this also was vanity... my heart still guiding me with wisdom—and how to lay hold on folly, till I might see what was good for the children of man to do under heaven during the few days of their life.*
>
> — Ecclesiastes 2:1, 3b

> *[He] took a journey into a far country, and there he squandered his property in reckless living.*
>
> — Luke 15:13

For the son to leave "for a distant country" indicates more than running away. The son is no wide-eyed George Bailey of Frank Capra's 1946 classic film *It's a Wonderful Life*, exclaiming, "I'm goin' shake this dust of this crummy little town off my feet and see the world!" Instead, the young son's request is not only disrespectful—"You're dead to me, pops… Your only value is in your death"—but a violent battle cry. He's defecting and beginning a great rebellion.

The son's radical request is "a heartless rejection of the home in which the son was born and nurtured."[1] He's drastically rejecting all that made him who he was. It's a betrayal of the values of his family and community, in faith and tradition, that is, all the ways of living with all the ways of thinking and behaving. It was the rejection of all the things beloved by the family and "handed down to him from generation to generation as a sacred legacy."[2] All that is valuable and trustworthy are rubbished as he makes his home in the distant country.

In essence, the son kills his father relationally, emotionally, and religiously. His radically shameful deed of murder reveals his callous heart—his resentfulness. There's not a shred of respect for the father. To the son, the father is nothing of value; only a roadblock to blow up, perhaps a thing of his creation which justified the will to kill it. In his ruthless criticism of religion and distorted forms of Christianity, Friedrich Nietzsche brings to life the attitude of the son. He writes:

> *Where did God go? I will tell you! We have killed Him—you and I! We are all His murderers! But how did we do this? How were we able to drink up the sea? Who gave us the sponge to wipe away the whole horizon?... God is dead!... And we have killed Him! [The most familiar thing that] the world has ever known has bled to death under our knives–who will wash this blood clean from our hands? With what water might we be purified?... Is not the greatness of this deed too great for us? Must we not become gods ourselves, if only to appear worthy of it?*[3]

Nietzsche speaks on behalf of most of the modern Western world about the supposed "freedom" experienced from God's "death." Although I disagree with Nietzsche's philosophy and assertions about

Christianity, there's the truth about how we, as humanity, have treated God as dead in the act of rebellion. In actuality, we're forsaking God and the image of Him within—our sonship. They are no longer of any value to us. To kill the image of God within us is to destroy the goodness and values placed there by God. Whatever is lovely, good, right, and acceptable is left behind.

Choosing liberation from God's domain in our passionate choice for knowing what's good and evil for ourselves is the very thing we find our first parents did in the book of *Genesis*, the record of beginnings:

> *And out of the ground the Lord God made to spring up every tree that is pleasant to the sight and good for food. The tree of life was in the midst of the garden, and the tree of the knowledge of good and evil... And the Lord God commanded the man, saying, "You may surely eat of every tree of the garden, but of the tree of the knowledge of good and evil you shall not eat, for in the day that you eat of it you shall surely die..." (Genesis 3:9; 16-17).*

> *[Satan said] "For God knows that when you eat of it your eyes will be opened, and you will be like God, knowing good and evil." So when the woman saw that the tree was good for food, and that it was a delight to the eyes, and that the tree was to be desired to make one wise, she took of its fruit and ate, and she also gave some to her husband who was with her, and he ate. Then the eyes of both were opened, and they knew that they were naked. And they sewed fig leaves together and*

> *made themselves loincloths… Then the Lord God said, "Behold, the man has become like one of us in knowing good and evil. Now, lest he reach out his hand and take also of the tree of life and eat, and live forever",*
> *therefore the Lord God sent him out from the garden of Eden to work the ground from which he was taken* (Genesis 3: 22-23).

Trusting in themselves to know what was good and delightful, Adam and Eve rid themselves of God's governance and presence. Therefore, although it pained Him, God sent them on their way to a different place, a distant land.

We find this same truth within Jesus' parable. The son believes that he would be better off with the freedom to taste for himself what is pleasant or distasteful. Adam and Eve, along with the prodigal son, have a passion for unconditionally accepting anything that looks pleasing to the eye. Why did they have to do this when they knew the truth about the fruit? Because they mistrusted their Father, thinking that He was holding out on them, reserving for Himself alone what was good. This is called unbelief, the act of suppressing the truth and exchanging it for a lie, failing to respect the purpose of life to live with God under His will (see Romans 1:18-25).

A Journal Entry: I Abandoned My Home in God

Today was the first time I've sat down to take account of my sins and my identity without God. Hosea 10:13, which the Spirit led me to, opened the eyes of my heart to the reality of how my sin works and how it contributes to the sin in the world:

You have plowed iniquity;

you have reaped injustice;

you have eaten the fruit of lies.

Because you have trusted in your way…way…

This is hard for me to accept. I've tried to distract myself from this reality. It's hurtful to see myself as one so unfaithful, one that is so flippant towards God and all that is Good. So I've had some defensive and reluctant emotions towards my life of sin.

I see that our sin issue is deep. It's a plague. The weight of sin is serious. I have been confused about why Adam and Eve could have declared their independence from God when they had everything without any pain or struggle. Are we so weak that we refuse to depend on God in even the best of situations? How is it we can have everything but say that God is holding out on us? Why are we so passive about evil, and why do we have contempt for God's governance? Why is it that we feel the need to be equal with God? Do we really believe that God doesn't know what's good for us? Or that He holds out on us?

My sin is not excusable; It's a willful war on God's will. And I've made myself ruler and judge for myself. Hiding my ways from my heart and skewed my understanding.

I have plowed iniquity and have reaped injustice. I have eaten lies and deserve its fruits. Because my ways have governed me, I've given authority to many things.

I was mournfully cut off from God's family. I've committed a serious crime. I'm a criminal in the courts of heaven for rebelling against the Father of all. I've taken on the name of Rebel.

How many times have I said no to God up to this point in life! It's time to talk to God about these choices. I feel so much shame about not having the proper hatred towards sin. I haven't even considered bringing my struggles before the Lord.

I delight myself in sin, worshiping at the altars of my pleasures. Self-gratification honors me. I give up on God when I feel pain, for a quick feel-good moment. I've invited ways to rebel against God, rejecting all that is good. I have had disdain for God's ways and His authority, crowning myself king. I have put a priority on my dedication to my work and pleasure. I've attributed life to illicit intimacies, given them power in my life that is not theirs. I have used God's name to carry out what I desire to justify them.

I did not keep myself in the presence of God but abandoned my home in God, my proper home. I was put in darkness, chained in doom. I rejected the Author of life to author my own. Now, I am in chains, and death awaits me. I can no longer go into God's presence and warmth.

I've desired more than the desires of God, and now I am disconnected from His blessings.

Before sin, God was my mighty deliverer and confidant, in whom I felt secure. In sin, God in His power is deemed to me to be a threat, like an enemy. My body seems to be my disgrace, not the miracle I once knew it as. I see that my heart knows little about what's good for me and is very confused. There seems to me to be a veil of smoke and cloud between God and me. I have forgotten who God truly is to me. His image is distorted. I no longer have the rest to enjoy His presence—just peril.

5 The Indecent Luxury of Rejection

Figure 5: *Judas Walking Away*

And the younger of them said to his father, "Father, give me the share of property that is coming to me." And he divided his property between Not many days later, the younger son gathered all he had and took a journey into a far country, and there he squandered his property in reckless living.

— **Luke 15:12-13**

But the Lord God called to the man and said to him, "Where are you?" And he said, "I heard the sound of you in the garden, and I was afraid, because I was naked, and I hid myself."

— **Genesis 3:9-10**

In Jesus' parable, the father's response to the younger son's indecent request is surprising. He fulfills it all by dividing his property. His weasel of a son receives his inheritance and then goes out and liquidates it all.

Liquidation would only be lawful after the father's death (the proceeds of future harvests would go to dad's retirement until he died). Meaning the younger son wasn't the only one being "indecent" in the parable. The father had to treat himself as dead to fulfill his son's request. No father in their right mind would have allowed his son to speak to him the way the young son did, let alone fulfill his requests to the letter. On top of this, he allows the son to stay home for several more days (hence the "Not many days later").

The narrative seems to suggest that the father is gifting the "indecent" gift of compassion to the son regardless of the son's blatant rejection. There's no argument recorded between the father and son, no sense of the father pulling back his arms from his son, withholding a blessing. Nor is there any inclination about the father trying to prevent his son from leaving—he hadn't forced his love on him in any way.

As Henry Nouwen suggests:

He had to let him go in freedom, even though he knew the pain it would cause both his son and himself. It was love itself that prevented him from keeping his son home at all cost. It was love itself that allowed him to let his son find his own life, even with the risk of losing it.[1]

Here, the mysterious veil of our lives is lifted. To reject God is to deny whom we belong with and our identity within that relationship.

Identity Crisis

In the parable, Jesus addresses the core experience of the two groups in His audience and all of humanity with the same concept: leaving home spiritually.

Out of the unconditional love of God, He gives us an indecent luxury to choose against Him: the ability to reject Him to search for our worth and identity. "Leaving home" is becoming deaf to the voice that calls us dearly loved and becoming numb to the sense that we belong.[2] It's sensing the acceptance and affection of God's blessing hands and hearing His voice but then listening to every other voice. These voices exclaim, "Get out of the home that you've mistaken for your own—go out and prove you are worth something!" They come in various forms—people, situations, advertisements, religion, university, etc. (whether directly or indirectly). Thus, leaving home is essentially our exchange of God's truth for a lie.

You can see that your proper self-image is that you've been created in the image of God (see Genesis 1:26-27). But we allow tradition, secular distortions, or anything else to keep us away from God's home, His truth. If your idea of your worth to God is wrapped up in the voices around you and not the voice of the Father, you'll never experience who you really are.

If we listen to self-commentaries or those voices of the world who say, "You're not worth anything unless you conform to the present image of what is beautiful and pleasing," our self-worth is destroyed. As a result, we become frustrated and resentful, not being the person we want to be to conform to the image of society. In confusion, we may perceive God to be a slave master keeping from us our potential. But the message of God is that He loves us and wants us, not because we are useful, but because He loves us.

To be at home is to embrace your complete self in love, taking God's side in the evaluation of you. Love for oneself is respect for oneself as a child of God. This is reserved for God's family and designed for fellowship with God.

When we have self-love in the sense of vanity, pride, and ego, it's not love. It's an illusion or a counterfeit love. That kind of feeling makes man an idol (see chapter six, page 52), a god to be worshiped rather than the one true God. Naturally, God will then become worthless to us, and His presence is re-named "oppression." No wonder we reject the image of God within when we have no respect for the One who gave it for us to carry! God's image within us is mistaken for an intruder who robs. We kill it. And we leave home, having left our first love (see Revelation 2:4).

Leaving Home

My initial question upon pondering this truth of us leaving home was, "How do I know that I've ever left home, to begin with? Because I've rarely felt at home. I've never had a strong sense of belonging. But what is home exactly?"

In essence, home is the place of sonship in Christ (see Romans 8:14-16). Leaving home is not foreign to my spiritual experience, regardless of what I might think. Leaving home isn't a form of philosophical inquiry or even an event bound to time and place that I can point to with gladness that it's all over now. It's a spiritual struggle, having chosen over and over again to leave home, a battle which Nouwen expressed as "a denial of the spiritual reality that I belong to God…"[3] Leaving home means ignoring the truth that God knows me, cares for me, and values me. It's the search for acceptance, as though I am without and must search elsewhere to find it. It's running away from the hands which bless me to search for love in distant lands. It's becoming deaf to the voice that calls us beloved to listen to another voice.[4] There's no greater tragedy in life than that. And it's the great tragedy of my life and of the lives of so many I cross paths with.

My sister once told me of a lady who came into her store buying expensive potting soil. The lady disclosed that the soil was for plastic petunias she placed in her yard. The only reason she did so was to make people believe that she had a green thumb, which they did, giving her affirmation year-round. Ever since, she insists on buying expensive potting soil, even if the purchase puts her in debt. That's putting her worth in what others say instead of how God sees her as His beloved.

Spiritually leaving home is ignoring God's image inside of us to fashion a self-image by the affirmations of others and our own "goodness." In his book *Abba's Child*, Brennan Manning discusses how when we live in this spiritual state, the inner voice whispers:

> *"You've arrived..." there is no truth in that self-concept. When [we] sink into despondency and the inner voice whispers, "You are no good, a fraud, a hypocrite, and a dilettante," there is no truth in any image shaped from that message."*[5]

To leave the voice of God is to listen to the many other voices heard, which are loud, seductive, and lavished with glimmering promises. "Go out, do something, and prove you're worth something, worthy of love." After the voice of God announced from heaven His beloved-ness and Sonship, Jesus immediately left to go into the desert where another voice spoke. It was satan (whose name literally means "the slanderer" or "the accuser" *) who opposed Jesus' Sonship by

---

* "The Devil" means in Greek "The Slanderer." "Devil" is not a name. Which is why in the Hebrew language the word "The" is in front of "Satan." "The Satan" means "the adversary." An adversary isn't for anything, but is against or anti-everything. Therefore, satan works through lies (counterfeits) to destroy us.

challenging Him to do something to prove Himself. There were three voices or temptations to prove His worthiness:

1. "If you are the Son of God, command this stone to become bread…"

2. "I will give you all their [the kingdoms of the world's] authority and splendor… If you worship me, it will all be yours,"

3. "If you are the Son of God, throw yourself down from here [this temple]. For it is written, 'He will command his angels concerning you to guard you carefully; they will lift you up in their hands so that you will not strike your foot against a stone.'" (Luke 4:1-12 NIV)

The first temptation concerns itself with receiving provision. The second is about obtaining power and favor. The third is about testing Jesus' worth, or His identity.

The voice of satan comes through various agents to coax us to leave our home. It must be this way, or we won't fall into his trap. People are different, and for temptations to be the most seductive, they must become tailored to their taste and situation. Notice how satan offered Jesus all of the worldly powers and pleasures He could have as a king through earthly means. When Jesus refused, satan gave a religious opportunity for power and prestige. While hearing the voices, Jesus identified as the Beloved Son of the Creator, already having provisions, power, favor, and worth. Satan knew who Jesus was but called for Him to obtain it Himself to prove His worthiness.

Leaving home shows itself as an indecent luxury that no

disciple can afford. It's the rejection of the truth that "I'm beloved" by following the voices which tell me to doubt my self-worth and prove myself. It's leaving home for the distant land believing that "I'm not going to be loved without having earned it through my efforts."[6]

"You're not acceptable until you do!" The voices demand. "Do everything and anything possible to gain acceptance."

Self-Rejection

Leaving home rejects who I am to the Father because the voices tell me that I'm not enough. This is self-rejection.

But to be worthy by being with, rather than by doing, is one of the unique claims of Christianity, setting it apart from religions. Almost every religion says we achieve wholeness and goodness—since we're not fundamentally broken—bettering ourselves as we do. The Bible, however, says we're in such a fractured state we can't improve ourselves or save ourselves by anything we do. So wholeness is only found in being with the One who delivers us from who we are and what we have done. And that One is Christ. Hours before being murdered, Christ prayed this prayer for unity:

> *...that they [believers] may all be one, just as you, Father, are in me, and I in you, that they also may be in us, so that the world may believe that you have sent me. The glory that you have given me I have given to them, that they may be one even as we are one, I in them and you in me, that they may become perfectly one, so that the world may know that you sent me and loved them even as you loved me. Father, I desire that*

they also, whom you have given me, may be with me where I am, to see my glory that you have given me because you loved me before the foundation of the world (John 17:21-24).

In every counterfeit religion, the enemy proclaims a way of growing by doing instead of entering the Dwelling of all Righteousness, our Lord Jesus Christ—the one who has done everything perfectly.* To reject our home is to abandon God and who we are fundamentally—the beloved. It's the trap of self-rejection. Of this great trap, Henry Nouwen shares,

> *I have come to realize that the greatest trap in our life is not success, popularity, or power, but self-rejection... When we have come to believe in the voices that call us worthless and unlovable, then success, popularity, and power are easily perceived as attractive solutions...*[7]

Self-rejection contradicts God's voice that calls us His sons and daughters. If our true spiritual life is expressed as being God's beloved, we must change our perception of ourselves to match His. Whether greater or less than the one God has of us, any other image of ourselves we adopt is a life of sin. Therefore, self-rejection is an indecent luxury no disciple can afford. Though God disapproves of sin (sin means "to miss the mark"—His mark), He will not withhold His compassion towards those who rely on His goodness, even if there are impurities within them.

---

* True and pure, religion before the True God is presented in James 1:27 as a lifestyle: taking care of the vulnerable and keeping oneself unstained from the world.

And so our Father weeps when we leave home driven by shame and self-hatred, moving away from His mercy. In our moment of losing self-compassion, we take cover in a distant country. We've learned to take part in this indecent luxury from our first parents, Adam and Eve, who hid from God because they didn't like what they saw in themselves (see Genesis 3:6-10). Like Adam and Eve, God calls us out of hiding, but we take cover behind anything that presents shade to hide our bare, naked, ugly selves. Therefore leaving home is not God leaving us, but us leaving God. Leaving home may not be out of our complete contempt for a compassionate God but fear for our inadequate self. I believe that many of us haven't lost faith in our Father but that we have more faith in the wretchedness of our inadequacies that disgust us. Though this doesn't mean that we may have acknowledged we're wretched, but that we put more effort in covering up than trusting God when we fail.

Our true self has its positives and negatives, and we tend to reject or remain ignorant of the least acceptable parts of us and our personality. Dr. Carl Jung called this elaboration by the sinister title of "The Shadow" or "The Shadow Self." It's the notion of how the shadow is central to the human condition and a part of our conscious self that it doesn't identify itself with. We've got to acknowledge our tendency to hide our darkness if we're going to have any relationship with God.

The younger son had a version of himself that was so distorted that it allowed him to think that his indecent request for his father's death was called for—within his rights. It makes me wonder how many times I act out of my dark side, going around afflicting people and God with my indecent requests. For the younger son, his self-rejection so far has manifested itself in arrogance. A little later in chapter seven, we see it on display in his low self-esteem.

6 The Law Of Addiction

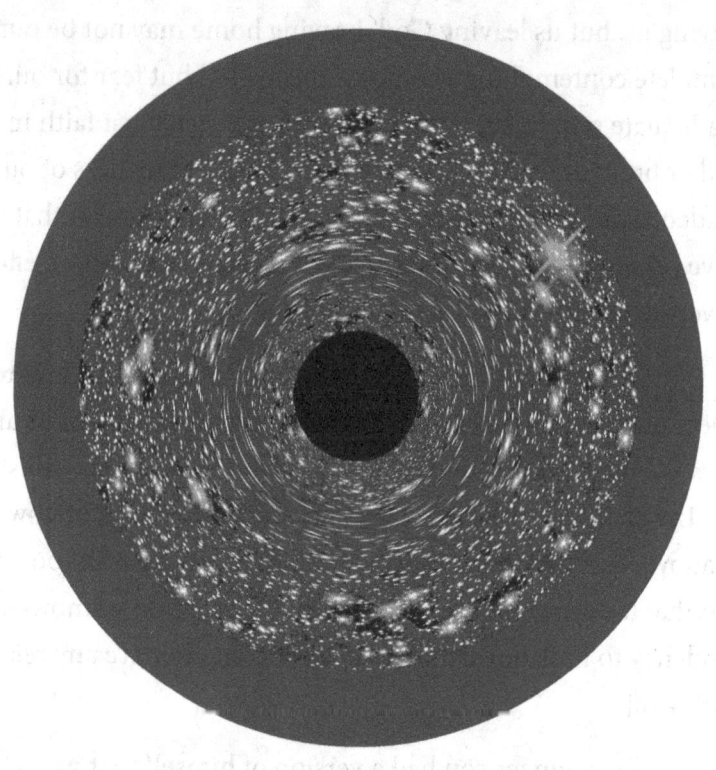

Figure 6: *Addiction Is A Behemoth Black Hole*

but they became futile in their thinking, and their foolish hearts were darkened. Claiming to be wise, they became fools, and exchanged the glory of the immortal God for images resembling mortal man…

— **Romans 1:21b-23a**

Woe to you, scribes and Pharisees, hypocrites! For you are like whitewashed tombs, which outwardly appear beautiful, but within are full of dead people's bones and all uncleanness.

— **Matthew 23:27**

Self-rejection isn't simply the irrational or drastic expression of an insecure person but the natural manifestation of a much deeper human darkness: The feeling of not being genuinely welcomed in human existence.[1] This is why addiction is so prevalent among us. Addiction may be defined as the tiresome search and struggle to discover the fullness of love. It's running around looking for someone or something to convince me that I belong, that I'm loved. Addiction is the eager attentiveness to every voice that doesn't come from God, voices who demand, "Prove your worth; do something relevant, spectacular, or powerful, then you'll earn and feel the love you desire."[2]

For me, addiction was catering to what I perceived were people's expectations, making sure I was always well-liked for what I did. It was overeating to feel at home. It was driving around at night, hoping it would give me a sense of "going" somewhere and leaving my problems behind. It was lying to pretend that I was different than who I was to get a pat on the back. It was buying 1,500 dollars worth of books each year, believing if I knew "everything," I could be respectable—people could give me the dignity I craved. Then, being accomplished, people would seek me, and I would find placement in the world.

The younger son expresses the law of addiction in Jesus' parable in Luke 15:13b. This verse literally translates from the Greek, "There he scattered thoroughly the substance of him living recklessly."[3] He's trading possessions of his old life for a new one in hopes of finding freedom and belonging. Here we have a son rejecting his family's acceptance to give himself to performance-based acceptability. We can rightfully ask, "Why would anyone trade a home of unconditional acceptance in exchange for a life in a performance-driven world resulting in conditional love?" It's a good question.

Consider this: When you're far away from home, what law do you live by? The law of the land, of course. Is it true of you, as it's of me, that you hope that some person, thing, or event will give you that final feeling of inner well-being, the full welcome and unconditional love you desire? That hope is the law of all addiction. It's the compulsive thought and disciplined pursuit of "Maybe it's this book, course, job; house, investment, car; relationship, church, drug, or this pint of double chocolate ice-cream that will fulfill my deepest longing."

Like the younger son, we, too, have been lured by deceitful voices of distant lands. We exchange parts of our true identity for glimmering promises of acceptance based on what we can do or have.

A Tale of Two Cities is a book most of us have heard of or even read. Charles Dickens wrote the book to state "his belief in the possibility of resurrection and transformation…"[4] By the main character delivering himself to the guillotine, he becomes a Christ-like figure in death serving to save the lives of others. Through his service, his life earns both worth and significance.[5] The supreme sacrifice "of his final act speaks to a human capacity for change," a belief that "sacrifice is necessary to achieve happiness."[6]

It's a universal idea that sacrifice is necessary for life to be lived with freedom. Throughout history, there are many people making sacrifices—but not many making the right ones. Have you noticed how many who make sacrifices, tend to end up in the ruins of sufferance, not significance?

The law of addiction is the misplaced compulsiveness to sacrifice; that thing that keeps us busy yet never getting anywhere but miserable and worn out with its glimpses of shallow happiness. It's why addiction is so demanding. It demands you to feed it and let it slumber before you have had your own. At the peril of your own will and healthy relationships, it tells you how to behave, what to say, and when to do its bidding. Addiction exists to own you, not to free you. It makes you its slave.

When we move away from home, listening to the voices that deny that love is an entirely free gift, we lose faith in the Voice that calls us sons and daughters. Not only that, but we sell ourselves out as slaves to every voice that offers a way to win the love we so desire.[7] This is why, as long as we wait for the elusive moment that we hope will give us that final feeling of inner well-being, full welcome, and complete love we desire, we'll always be anxious, depressed, envious, and angry. All the while still enslaved to our disappointment and fears. Perhaps this is why Jesus tells us to go and learn what this means when He directs us to the words, "I DESIRE COMPASSION, RATHER THAN SACRIFICE" (Matthew 9:13 NASB). Paul understood Jesus' words when he wrote, "For you have not received a spirit of slavery leading to fear again, but you have received a spirit of adoption as sons and daughters by which we cry out, 'Abba! Father!'" (Romans 8:15 NASB).

The parable of *The Prodigal Son* exemplifies the words of Jesus and Paul. It's the tale of two spirits, one of compassion, one of sacrifice.(Chapters ten and eleven talk about these spirits or attitudes towards life and God.)

"There can only be two basic loves," wrote Augustine of Hippo, "the love of God unto the forgetfulness of self, or the love of self unto the forgetfulness and denial of God."[8] These are fundamental choices at the core of our being. Our choice is made real in the choices we make in daily life. It's a choice of adoption or slavery. It's either being attached to self-importance, being tossed back and forth by egocentric desires, or resting in the reality that I'm highly favored by my Father regardless of what I do or don't do.

Our constant need for the favor of man reminds me of the comic yet philosophical film *Zelig*. It has the form of a solemn documentary about the life of Leonard Zelig, a popular fictional character who perfectly fits in everywhere because he changes his personality constantly to match each changing situation.

> *He has no personality of his own, so he assumes whatever strong personalities he meets up with. With the Chinese, he is straight out of China. With rabbis, he miraculously grows a beard with side curls. With psychiatrists, he apes their jargon, strokes his chin with solemn wisdom… He wears a Yankee uniform in spring training and stands in the on-deck circle to bat after Babe Ruth… He is a "chameleon." He changes… as the world about him changes. He has no ideas or opinions of his own; he simply conforms. He wants only to be safe, to fit in, to be accepted, to be liked… He is famous for being nobody, a nonperson.[9]*

Although Zelig is a grandiose caricature of the traditional people pleaser, the classic codependent, or an illusory person, we shouldn't dismiss Zelig as something merely fictional. Zelig is very much alive and well in our daily lives whenever we adopt a "radical poseur of our egocentric desires" that "wears a thousand masks."[10]

It's a never-ending cycle of living out of a compulsive desire to hide behind perfect images so that everyone may admire us and nobody will know us.[11]

Through social conditioning, the false self with its many layers, a false image on top of another false image, adheres to the individual so closely to the point they are wrapped as like an onion. The true self is mummified. There comes the point where the true self and the false self seem indistinguishable, both to the host and the viewer. The false self makes us live in a world of delusion, and that's why, to all intents and purposes, "the imposter prompts us to attach importance to what has no importance, clothing with a false glitter that is least substantial."[12]

As Gerald May noted, "It is important to recognize these self-commentaries for the mind tricks they are. They have nothing to do with our real dignity. How we view ourselves at any given moment may have very little to do with who we really are."[13] May tells us that addiction closely follows and feeds these self-commentaries, enslaving ourselves to the gods we create. We no longer listen to the all-powerful, all-knowing, all-loving Father calling us beloved but are listening to every voice that persuades us to be preoccupied with powerless vanities.

James Masterson wrote in *The Search for the Real Self* how the powerless images and vanities we hold onto "plays its deceptive role, ostensibly protecting us" from our shadow self, "but doing so in a way that is programmed to keep us fearful—of being abandoned, losing support, not being able to cope with our own, not being able to be alone."[14] When becoming caught up in attributing power to powerless vanities, we fall into some kind of hysterics. We become fearful of being stripped of the images we have created because we have made them into things that can bring us "life." Although empty of life themselves, they "protect" us from the nothingness we are. Therefore, when there's the absence of the vanities we depend on for meaning, they become to us an object of death—rejection. (Attributing power to that which is powerless and the experience of its "protection" and "power" it has over us in our fear [although making us weaker] reminds me of the notion of idolatry, the concept which originated in Judaism.)

Such revelation comes to mind when reading the story of a patient of the famous psychologist Carl Jung. The patient struggled with chronic depression, and Jung told the patient to spend his evenings in his study, quiet and all alone. The patient did what he understood Jung to have advised. After an eight-hour workday (reduced from his fourteen hours), the patient closed the door to his study, sat down, and read classic works with a few Chopin études or some Mozart. After a few weeks of this, he returned to Jung, expressing deep frustration about the practice not being therapeutic. When Jung heard how the patient used his time, he responded, "But you didn't understand. I didn't want you to be with Hasse or Mann nor Chopin or Mozart. I wanted you to be completely alone." The man, now more annoyed, exclaimed, "I can't think of any worse company." Jung replied, "Yet this is the self you inflict on other people fourteen hours a day."[15]

Although somewhat a comedic response by Jung, there's a more profound truth in his words, and that's the reality of how we hide in an attempt to keep from inflicting ourselves and others with our real self. Jung thought of this hiding act as part of the human condition.

I know this to be true of me. I don't remember experiencing freedom as a child unless I was doing something. I always felt internal pressure. There was someone to be or something to do. So when I found myself alone, I was unsatisfied with the present and unhappy with myself. Constantly feeling disappointed, sad, lonely—in the gutter—it was painful to know who I indeed was, so my relief was trying to be anything else, even if my striving led to a poor ending.

Everyone is shadowed by an illusory person—a false self—some image of a perfect person we hide behind for everyone to admire, rather than have the unacceptable parts of our true self exposed.[16] The ability to expose and deal with the false self constitutes a challenging endeavor as it's neither something one eagerly confronts nor accepts as present within them. We're willfully blind to our illusory self's existence as we paint and camouflage it in a painful attempt to project an image, although false, to fit the narrative about ourselves that we espouse.

The false self is enamored and obsessed with the size of our wounds and makes sure to cover our nothingness with bandages of glittering images. With wounds covered, we forget their existence—and gangrene sets in. This kind of behavior is what John Bradshaw defines as a disease "characterized by a loss of identity... out of touch with one's feelings, needs, and desires."[17] (This loss of identity is something we'll talk about in chapter seven.)

The false self advocates "to seem to be" rather than "to be;" therefore, the "seeming to be" becomes its mode of operation.

I'm preoccupied with my weight. If I binge on a pint of double-chocolate ice cream and see the scales in the morning tilted the wrong way, I'm crushed. I've become preoccupied with my performance at work. One word of criticism, and I feel utterly rejected as an incompetent jerk with no significance. Of course, my objections to such preoccupations are met with rationalizations of how "A fat one won't be accepted as a legit leader," or "A university degree is required if you want to be respected."

The façade we build keeps the false self stable—makes us feel safe. But it's easily dismantled when reality doesn't match up to what we believe about ourselves. The safety found in a life lived through the illusory person can quickly turn into disorientating chaos, leading us into neurosis, erratic behavior, and drastic measures to avoid the nothingness and powerlessness of ourselves. It's what we call addiction.

Nouwen beautifully shares in his book *The Return of the Prodigal Son* his preoccupation with acceptance and love:

> *As long as I keep running about asking: "Do you love me? Do you really love me?" I give all power to the voices of the world and put myself in bondage because the world is filled with "ifs." The world says: "Yes, I love you if you are good-looking, intelligent, and wealthy. I love you if you have a good education, a good job, and good connections. I love you if you produce much, sell much, and buy much." There are endless "ifs" hidden in the world's love. These "ifs" enslave me since it is impossible to respond adequately to all of them.*[18]

The world's love is and always will be "if"—condition-based. It gives birth to addictions because what it offers cannot satisfy our hearts' deepest pangs of hunger. As long as we keep looking for our true self in the world of conditional love, we'll remain addicted to the world—trying, failing, and trying again.[19]

An incredible amount of time, energy, and money are devoted to the fitness and dietary aid industries. Some of the most recognized magazines, books, apps, services, courses, and even scientific debates relate to getting and staying in the shape of the Instagram celebrities or the Calvin Klein models. Every program becomes followed, every device bought, and every calorie counted. The market is saturated with personal trainers who gain an average annual salary of 50+k. What's spiritual wholeness compared to the pleasures of having rock-hard abs or a full and firm butt and even being an expert in achieving them?

The imposter attaches power and significance to the most trivial and unimportant things. No wonder Apostle Paul warned his protégée, Timothy, "for a while bodily training is of some value, godliness is of value in every way, as it holds promise for the present life and also for the life to come" (1 Timothy 4:8). We must be careful not to place confidence in a thing or practice as infallible techniques for acquiring good things. If we do, we'll find cheap worth that costs us everything.

I find what Thomas Merton said to be appropriate here: "A life devoted to the shadow is a life of sin."[20] Everyone at some point devotes their life to the illusionary. If you are like me, you have been loyal to vanities, then found yourself having left them, only to return again.

Like the younger son, we too have been lured by deceitful voices of distant lands. We exchange parts of our true identity for glimmering promises of acceptance based on what we can do or have. We labor and slave away, being distant from the acceptance we left, which was full of the riches of grace. The wealth of God's grace becomes unaccepted by our lack of embrace towards the reality of our incompleteness without the Father. We're holding onto pride, trying to prove our greatness, and because of it, we're squandering a beautiful spiritual life filled with riches for a life of addiction. Many of us today, including those who are Christians, vehemently believe the need to earn our way, maybe even having to earn our way to Heaven—to merit salvation. We've ignored or forgotten the tender Voice that speaks of our beloved-ness amid loud voices of a world that operates on a performance-based system. In turn, we're rejecting our spiritual families in our desire for independence, as if we're our own saviors.

A Journal Entry: My Struggle With Self-Rejection

My distorted and maimed image of personal failure and inadequacy led to a loss of self-compassion, triggering episodes of heavy depression, rage, addiction, and anxiety. If you'd have met me six years ago, you probably wouldn't imagine I could say, "There's something very wrong with me."

Son of a Christian missionary, I decided to go off to Bible college after being home-educated. After two years of biblical studies, I transferred to a university where I received my Bachelor's in Applied Science, graduating Magna Cum Laude. I was bummed out that I didn't graduate valedictorian; to me, it was evident that I wasn't smart or didn't try hard enough. However, the university professors did vote to award me with the Stone-Campbell Promising Scholar Award, meaning the university thought I would most likely do the best in academics.

That thought excited me, not because I enjoyed academics but because someone recognized me as someone who did well and would do well. Although many encouraged me to pursue graduate studies, I refused. In my mind, the luster of obtaining a graduate degree didn't outweigh its demand to be perfect, followed by the possibility of receiving crushing shame for not receive an *A*, if not failing studies completely. See, during and after receiving home education in youth, I believed that I was too dumb and inadequate for a competitive world.

After graduation, I sent out fifteen job applications accompanied by an excellent reference. All but three were rejected. My already low self-esteem dived. I was too young. Too experienced or too non-experienced. I ended up taking a pastoral job at a small, struggling country church in Virginia. I believe most people thought I took the job out of the "kindness of my heart." Although it was a fact that I liked helping struggling communities, I acted on my assumption that there are fewer expectations for success in such places.

After a year, the church was growing; but I was withering away. Most congregants treated me like Moses of the Bible, leading the Hebrews into the promised land. Many were excited, thinking the little church was going to be the place to be at. I was the guy whom people introduced their friends to if they had a need or a problem. It was always, "Come and meet my minister. He's great. I have never heard anyone preach and explain the Bible the way he does," or "He has shiny black shoes and wears a tie. He's professional." (Yeah, that was what was said.) People were right; I was a professional doer. It was hard not to be prideful, and in many ways, I was. I tried to live up to people's opinions that I could do no wrong. Everyone thinking well of me was most important to me; I would kill myself for it.

Doing two services and two teaching/group-therapy sessions, meeting with upset people, the elderly, the hospitalized, officiating funerals, setting up for church services, counseling individuals, and doing a lot of the administrative work, I was exhausted and stressed out. It wasn't really what I was doing that overwhelmed me, but it was why and how I was doing them. Everything had to be perfect, and I felt responsible for everything, anything, and everyone. This mindset seems inherent within most churches of the Restoration Movement, although unrealized. (Ironically, this mindset goes against a foundational Restoration belief that there's no distinction between clergy and laity, and everyone is responsible for serving.) Folks tended to act that if something went wrong, it was my problem. Maybe I hadn't caused the problem, but it was still my problem if the situation continued. If they didn't believe that, then I certainly did.

The "I'm the problem" mindset had spread into my relationships with the congregants. Having done pottery professionally, I was approached by one gentleman from the church, who purchased a decent amount of pottery from me, paying by a check. I lost the check. When I told the man what had happened, he quickly remarked that what I "did" was not "cool." He was agitated. Not wanting our relationship to suffer, I told him to consider the pottery a gift; have it on me. The following Sunday morning, he refused my gift, telling me I needed to be taught responsibility. His punishment for me? He paid me the amount minus the "canceling check" fee he paid his bank. He made sure I knew what he had done, writing the amount he deducted for his inconvenience.

I recall a deacon I had phoned who chewed me out for not answering his phone call that morning. I explained that I hadn't a record of him calling me, most likely due to the lousy cell service connection in the remote hills. He interrupted, screaming, "Young man, you need some teaching on how to minister right. You can't do your job well because you're an incompetent youth. I'll teach you a lesson right now!" I did some screaming back like a big child I became when feeling pushed around.

Although petty, unrealistic complaints and beliefs did come way too often, and I couldn't realize them as such in the moment. The negative encounters with people were little things, but it was just an example of people being unwilling to extend human dignity to me in any way. These growing situations left me wondering if I deserved basic human dignity at all. People's un-compassionate remarks and actions always seemed to me like a threat equal to death. Weirdly, I began to believe I was a terrible human being, "Maybe everyone is right; I can't do anything right. Maybe I am the problem. I need to do better."

Trying to perform better meant keeping up with everyone's expectations, which I soon found out was utterly impossible. Working with people, and especially church people (specifically people who think they do most things right because they attend church services), can be exhausting.

I vividly recall blowing up in front of my class one Sunday morning after a man challenged me with a demanding question. From then on, even after a public apology and even going to each person's home asking for forgiveness, some of my significant supporters in the ministry stopped supporting me. Some wanted nothing to do with me or anything I had to say. Warm hugs turned to cold shoulders. This crushed me. I remember apologizing to one lady for my demand for respect. She, right after, told me how wrong I was... as if I had never apologized with an already broken spirit. I gently pointed this out and reaffirmed how sorry I was, but she responded that I only provided more evidence for how cruel and demanding I was. I couldn't forgive myself, and religious people reminded me that I was unforgivable.

As things became more performance-based in the church, migraines became a reoccurring experience, along with my self-disgust. I went to the emergency room many times, with plenty of doctor visits afterward. Unfortunately, nothing seemed to help the migraines.

Meanwhile, I'd packed on 60 pounds. I felt disgusting, and people reminded me of that weekly with comments like, "You have gained a lot. You're so fat now. I almost don't recognize you." I cared what people thought of me. My weight and eating habits were always a touchy subject. I was embedded with shame as an 11-year-old when I was at a public event that involved eating homemade Christmas baked goods. Seeing me stuff several cookies in my mouth and failing to balance the tower of brownies and cookies on my two hands, a relative told me, "You need to stop that. People are watching you. You're a Christian." Forget about why I was gluttonous because the issue was being gluttonous—the behavior only! I slowly learned from others that what people saw you do crafted their value of you.

My first two girlfriends shamed me for my extra poundage even while I was losing pounds and eating restrictively. My soon-to-be fiancée and I were 48 hours away from purchasing our rings when she told me she found me unattractive and couldn't see herself consummating the marriage we planned. She later told me that it would help her feel more attracted to me if I was less physically and emotionally present. She expressed it right after she said, "I wish you were more physical and emotional with me." I was confused; how could I be wrong for always being "with" her yet be bad at the same time for not always being "with" her? Six days later, she broke up with me, saying that she knew that "us" wouldn't work; she knew this even when we agreed to marry; it was "just" a feeling she had. I did everything I could to please her and promised to try to do better. But it didn't help. Going from "You're more than the perfect man I ever dreamed for; let's get married" to "I always feel wrong about the relationship, I don't want to be with you," I felt betrayed. All I heard her communicating was, "Thomas, whatever you do is not good enough for me to be with you." The last words spoken to me were,

"The four dozen flowers you bought for me are in that pottery vase you made to keep in the family. Well, I don't want to take the flowers out, so how much do I owe you?" All very hurtful.

That's when I had my first suicide attempt, having to stay in a mental ward for three days. After that, the doctors told me I was able to return to work. So I did.

After five days of returning, I preached on a Sunday. The following day, I called a meeting with some of the men of the church. When I arrived at my own meeting, I was asked to leave and return in an hour. When I returned, I was met at the door by five men with crossed arms who later told me they didn't want me or my family to visit the church or talk to anyone at the church for three months. They said they needed healing for the mess I had dragged them through. One stated, "No one has ever told you that this world is not about you." ("Great words" for someone who just attempted suicide.) Oddly enough, they were surprised when I handed in my resignation.

7 Purgatory: An Affair With *Do*

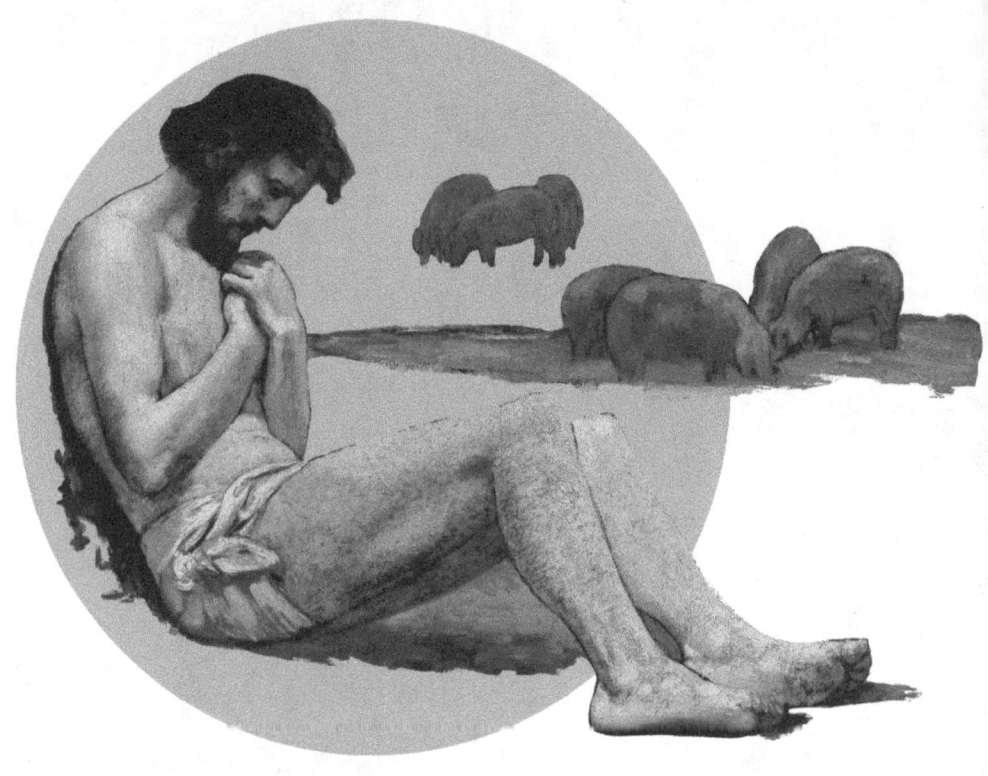

Figure 7: *The Prodigal's Purgatory*

Therefore God gave them up in the lusts of their hearts to impurity, to the dishonoring of their bodies among themselves, because they exchanged the truth about God for a lie...

— **Romans 1:24-25a**

When you've emptied your pockets for cheap worth, and there's no support, the tragedy radically alters your direction. You have to choose between death or life. It's the reality the young prodigal faces. He experiences an impoverished life in the distant land of glimmering promises of untold wealth.

The son is bankrupt, and now there's a famine. If he went bankrupt during the drought, you and I could sympathize, right? We know how quickly money goes to expenses and yesterday's debt. Building an emergency fund comes after paying off debt, so, many never have one. But as a recent heir, the son shouldn't be bankrupt. But he is. And there's famine in that country, nowhere else. The distant land no longer looks able to deliver on what it promised the young man. The prodigal's search for life outside the home now places him in a diminished reality.

The distant land is ruthless in offering what it doesn't have. It's bankrupt of anything of substantial value. But once there, addictions take hold, and we make a stronghold of what culture proclaims to be the "answer" to all wholeness. Wealth, power, the attainment of status and affirmation, the excessive consumption of food and drink, and sexual gratification based on lust all "create expectations that cannot but fail to satisfy our deepest needs."[1] But as long as we live by the world's ways, our addictions banish us from a fulfilled life, sending us down into a miserable, futile, and sometimes fatal life in the "distant country."

Busy Going Nowhere

The hallmark of the distant country is how you're busy going nowhere. The words of the Red Queen in Lewis Carroll's book *Through the Looking-Glass* seem apt: "Now, here, you see, it takes all the running you can do, to keep in the same place."[2] There're no advantages to living here. Each addiction here becomes pitted against the ever-evolving unhappiness and increasing nothingness we experience. Such a demanding lifestyle shows us that life in a distant land is, at best, a struggle for survival—the direct result of living as if what I do and own define me.[3]

The more we become entangled in the world's affairs, manipulations, and power games, the further we are from being at home. Everything leaves you with nothing. If you have ever been away from home, it's easy to identify with the words of Nouwen: "I try hard to please, to achieve success, to be recognized… I become suspicious or defensive and increasingly afraid that I won't get what I so much desire or will lose what I already have."[4]

When insecurities feel everywhere, it "culminates in the absolute meltdown" of the prodigal life we all live, says John MacArthur.[5]

The prodigal's quest for life outside of the home now appears to have become his imprisonment. If he felt being under the authority of his father was bondage, he finds the enslavement to his desires to be a more horrific existence. In his naïveté, the son hadn't considered all the dangers that lived there. He had acted out of impulse. Being a pleasure seeker, he gave no thought to getting established. The truth is, pleasure-seekers rarely think far ahead. And so, his sudden downfall was inevitable: "And when he had spent everything… he began to be in need."

MacArthur wonderfully examines the situation of the son's downfall, and ours alike: "Sin never delivers what it promises, and the pleasurable life [we] think [we] are pursuing always turns out to be precisely the opposite: a hard road that inevitably leads to ruin and the ultimate, literal dead end."[6] In a way, the prodigal and all those who squander like him become like Peter Pan, a lost boy of Neverland, being everything but nothing at the same time.

Dirty Deeds

Having left the bonds of grace that grow with interest, the prodigal is unemployed, homeless, and without a friend's couch to sleep on. Whatever "friends" and "connections" he found in his pursuit of happiness are absent now. I can imagine that when the boy had nothing else to give, his friends rejected him. When you're broke with nothing "useful," in people's minds, you're dead to them. He didn't want to work with dad, and he didn't work in the distant land. But now, he sets out to hire himself out.

Whatever status the prodigal had is gone, and so is an opportunity for a respectable job. Unfortunately, he can't find a regular job, only the lowest of all jobs in that day: a pig farmer's hired hand (the Jewish folk treated pigs with utter contempt). A dream job is no longer obtainable, and neither is the life he dreamed of. He stands powerless in the world's games. So he ends up feeding pigs.

Hearing of the son's new occupation probably generated quite a stir within Jesus' audience. The religious scoff, "That's what he deserves! Serves him right!" And everyone else is wide-eyed, "Ahh, pigs!" This is an emotional story, but no one is crying for the son's tragedy—after all, he's a prodigal.

Of the son's decision, MacArthur observes: "He thought he could pick himself up—maybe even work his way out of the dilemma. That is typical of [us when] on the run from God."[7] He further spirals into lostness by taking on this disgusting program of serving muddy pigs. See how he's still living in the distant country. Reassuring himself with the idea—his delusion—that he has the means and the ability to work his way out of the mess he had made of his life, he stays.[8]

This is what everyone initially does in a life of rebellion, even when depleted of resources, living in the ditches and sidewalks of life. An avoidance of repentance—the turning around to face the Father—is the life lived in pride. To be sure, if the prodigal had known of his now realized circumstances, he would've never left dad's side. But in pride, he's motivated by the obdurance of sinners, a state which seems impossible to explain rationally.[9] In pride, we're like the prodigal, still holding onto our most favorite delusions, sins, false images, and self-commentaries, even though we lay in the grave which they dug for us. We're still not quite ready to consider returning home. It's too embarrassing. We refused to be real before God because the false self dreads discovering itself to be nothing.

Since the false self claims to be everything, being left with nothing to do but its nothingness would mean its death.[10]

The Prodigal As A Codependent

In opposition to returning home, the prodigal had somehow found this pig farmer who had the privilege of citizenship (citizens were usually very wealthy [Roman] foreigners in that time). We're told in the Greek text that he "glued" himself to the citizen.* One could make the case that the prodigal son is officially showing himself as an unhealthy dependent, affixing himself to the closest person he knew for any significance. In an article from the book *Co-Dependency, An Emerging Issue*, Robert Subby defines unhealthy dependency as:

> *an emotional, psychological, and behavioral condition that develops as a result of an individual's prolonged exposure to, and practice of, a set of oppressive rules— rules which prevent the open expression of feeling as well as the direct discussion of personal and interpersonal problems.*[11]

Earnie Larsen, speaks of unhealthy dependency as "those self-defeating, learned behaviors or character defects that result in a diminished capacity to initiate or to participate in loving relationships."[12] We could very well say the prodigal has experienced the diminished capacity to initiate or participate in loving relationships in the distant land, resulting in his attachment to his boss.

---

* The Greek text employs a very picturesque verb: κολλάω, which literally means "to glue."

Perhaps he's taking comfort in slaving away in the muck and mire in being in an employee/boss relationship, rather than being a son, at home, with jewels upon his head. The reason I say this is because of how I see this in myself as a codependent. "A codependent person is one who has let another person's behavior affect him or her, and who is obsessed with controlling that person's behavior… codependents are reactionaries," shares Melody Beattie.[13]

If the world in the day of the prodigal was anything like today, I think he's taking comfort here in a contractual relationship having been scorned by others for being himself.

Here's a natural question that comes to mind: Why does anyone settle for a life in such a diminished form? Masterson answers our question by sharing how the nature of our false self tries to "save us from knowing the truth about our real selves from penetrating the deeper causes of our unhappiness, from seeing ourselves as we truly are—vulnerable, afraid, terrified and unable to let our real selves emerge…"[14] Not surprisingly, in our false self's defensiveness against our true feelings, needs and wants, our need for intimacy is sacrificed.[15] It's like how a baby may scream in need of her mother's milk, yet unfortunately, receives a blow to the face. The baby learns to detect what would elicit such disapproval—don't express the need for milk. How tragic!

Although the false self promises to serve you in connecting you with people, you'll not be able to experience intimacy in any relationship.[16] Not only does the pride and self-focus of our illusory person exclude others, but it puts you out of touch with your true self and estranges you from the human experience out of fear—your feelings, thoughts, and yearnings are ignored. We're caught in a tangle of wants and needs, no longer knowing our own motivations. The truth is, if you are not connected with yourself, you will lose all connection with others and with God. Tragically, we're confused, thinking, *I wonder why I lack intimacy with my community and God?*

Perhaps this is why the prodigal believed he deserved nothing less than to live in the pigpen. As Nouwen accurately suggests, "When no one wanted to give him the food he was giving to the pigs, the younger son realized that he wasn't even considered a fellow human being."[17] The son experiences reproach and estrangement as a fellow human being. No one welcomes him into their home. To be sure, the son would've thought his father would surely never welcome him back home. Welch defines the process well, "When you receive… reproach from the community, you can easily believe that God, Himself, joins those many voices, though he certainly does not."[18]

We've felt such separation throughout moments and events of life, haven't we? It's the loneliness that comes from losing all sense of having things in common with fellow humans. Through sharing something in common like background, values, religion, and education; connections, habits, traditions, age, and profession, there's a basis for acceptance. It's why when meeting a new person, the normal progression of conversation goes to these things. When I say, "I'm from Southside Virginia," the response is often "Oh, I have a friend who lives close to there," or "Oh, bet there are many cows where you live!" It's a mutual search for a common link, and when there are fewer things in common, the more distance we feel. We feel out of place, without a home. We become a lost foreigner. We not only feel like an outcast, but we are one. Unfortunately, we adopt it as our spiritual identity too.

Being unable to live from our authentic self is our particular dilemma and no one else's. We must learn to accept our deep-rooted desire to still operate out of a fear-based center. It's odd. But, isn't it true that when a person finds themselves away from home, they're away from the voice of God which proclaims their beloved-ness? It's why the son, like many of us, forgets where he belongs.

You've Earned Your Beans, So Eat Them

We're told that while in the pigpen, the son "came to himself" or "came to his senses." The son was sensing his starvation in more than one way—absolute brokenness. When the son was treated as less than human by people around him, the loss of human dignity woke him up. Having experienced total alienation, he came to his senses. He was becoming aware of the nothingness of his state and the road to death he was on. All he had known that gave him abundant life was far gone: family, friends, and community. Being disconnected from such life-giving sources, the son "realized that death would be the natural next step."[19] The threat of impending death is within his thin body. And now, he desires even the stiff, leathery leaflets of the swine pod (Carob bean) to stay alive. The free gifts of family, friends, and the community reminded the son of his beloved-ness and were life-giving for him. But desiring beans reserved for animals and hard times reminded him of reaping what he was sowing: death. (In Catalonia, you can still hear the expression, "to earn your carob-beans," meaning to "earn a wage.")[20]

Jesus' parable of the prodigal demonstrates what Apostle Paul later taught the churches in Rome about spiritual death:

- For the wages of sin is death, but the free gift of God is eternal life in Christ Jesus our Lord (Romans 6:23).

- For if you live according to the flesh, you will die, but if by the Spirit you put to death the deeds of the body, you will live (Romans 8:13).

Don't Let Your Nothingness Absorb You

When we live in the pigpen of our nothingness, our lostness confronts us, and we either wallow in it or opt-out. If we wallow, we'll lose touch with the divine image in which we are made. It's when you can no longer hold onto part of the Divine Image in which you were created. It's like what Nouwen shares:

> *This happens over and over again whenever I say to myself: "I am worthless. I am unlovable. I am a nobody." There are always countless events and situations that I can single out to convince myself and others that my life is just not worth living, that I am only a burden, a problem, a source of conflict, or an exploiter of other people's time and energy.*[21]

Being distracted from healing—redemption—many follow the dark voices which say, "I am no good. People are no good. Life is miserable and meaningless." This is a type of death. Naturally, that which does not bring us life, brings us death. Death is, of course, found in the desires of the distant land and life spent apart from the Father. Death is experienced as a curse. That happens whenever we feel remotely rejected from receiving what we deeply desire: acceptance. The reversal of acceptance is shame. Welch defines shame as "the deep sense that you are unacceptable because of something you did, something done to you, or something associated with you. You feel exposed and humiliated."[22] Our encounters with shame are like encounters with death. The withdrawal of acceptance—shame/death—is perceived or felt by all people differently because our backgrounds have sown unique insecurities.

Because of this, we must safeguard that little piece of God's image still inside of us that we do not give way to despair.[23] Although we must be cautious against being wholly absorbed in our brokenness, we also must guard against becoming distracted from the wounds we want to heal.

Rediscovery Of Self

The darkest moment of the prodigal's life afforded him with the opportunity to realize where he was headed—death—and choose against it. It was the moment that he rediscovered himself. I find fascinating the phrase "he came to himself." It's a sign of the act of coming in. The Greek phrase in its context shows this event as a turning of the heart in the wake of discovery (see Acts 12:11 and 1 Kings 8:47). Maybe for the first time in his life, the son was inviting himself to go home to the center of his being. In his reflection of his broken state, he came to a posture of understanding. As the text shows, he does so by talking with himself, as most do when things go amiss. Have you ever been known to talk out loud when you're really trying to work things out, and no one is around?

His choice to listen, to pay attention to his needs, in quiet contemplation is quite a feat given how the false self "flees silence and solitude which remind him of death."[24] The son is putting to death every identity not of God, facing his mortality and weakness. The word's of Thomas Merton reveal what the son could have said to himself:

> *There is no substance under the things with which I am clothed. I am hollow, and my structure of pleasures and ambitions has no foundation. I am objectified in them. But they are all destined by their very contingency to be destroyed. And when they are gone, there will be nothing left of me but my own nakedness and emptiness and hollowness...*[25]

Tragedy radically changes the direction of our lives because it would seem that by them, God's voice confronts us with a choice. It's the same voice which spoke to the Israelites on the verge of crossing the depths of the Jordan River to Canaan:

> *I call heaven and earth to witness against you today, that I have set before you life and death, blessing and curse. Therefore choose life, that you and your offspring may live, loving the Lord your God, obeying his voice and holding fast to him, for he is your life and length of days, that you may dwell in the land that the Lord... gives them* (Deuteronomy 30:19-20).

According to this passage, to choose life is to choose God. As Nouwen writes, "Indeed, it is a question of life or death. Do we accept the rejection of the world that imprisons us, or do we claim the freedom of the children of God? We must choose."[26]

Experiencing belonging, strength, dignity, and love is life for everyone. But, being deprived of such gifts, we experience shame—death.

This moment of contemplation marks the realization of the son's choices against his home that lead to death, making him choose life. His reflection upon the curses he's subjected to in the distant land, and the reminder that there's no blessing apart from life at home marks the son's choice to live. The son has started in the right direction, being humbled—but not utterly humiliated by his state. Although still distant, he's feeling a touch of blessing while embracing his brokenness by pondering life with the father again. Even so, his aim is still off the mark. He claims to be his father's son in his desire to return home, but we will see that he still desires servanthood.

A Journal Entry: My Encounter With Death

After my first suicide attempt, I jotted in my journal a list when trying to encourage myself to choose life. I wrote *My Reasons to Live*:

- My family would be devastated.

- I would be a perfect husband to a woman who is madly in love with me.

- I need to be an incredible father to children who change the world.

- I will be a leader in my field of work.

- I will be a noted craftsman in pottery.

- Experiencing sex would be great.

- I must preach the gospel and make disciples (this is my mission in life).

In looking back, my list is a bit crazy. I reached a point that I questioned how bulletproof my list was. OK. *What happens if I am not an incredible dad? If my kids are lousy, what then? I will obviously not be a perfect husband. And my wife will not always express mad love for me. So, then, what happens after? To be a leader in my field is pretty ambitious. When I don't live up to that, or lose my job, am I going to say all is lost? Ha. What about when I don't get married and have to live without sex. Is life a waste then? Oh. What if I make for a lousy Christian or don't witness to droves of people? Am I then a failure? To be sure, being a dad, a husband, a good potter or speaker, or even making disciples can be accomplished by anyone, not just me. So all of these are not good reasons to live for because they show me that I can merely be replaced.* Remember that I lost an engagement with a lady, besides losing my job, respect in my work field (though temporary), and being a lousy Christian.

Unfortunately, and ironically, my reasons to live began my experience of death all over again. This led to my second attempt at suicide.

Afterward, I realized that the list of "reasons to live" was really everything I thought life was found. I would experience life when I was married. Life would be felt in the birth of my child. Life would be found in the intimate acts of those married. Life was feeling great about my work, and feeling strong. Naturally, in the absence of those, I would only experience death. This is why feelings and desires for outside "life-support" cripple me, maim, and "kill" me.

Knowing all this, I became resolved to set my heart on things that didn't demand my perfection in performance—the grace and love of God.

8 Change of Heart

Figure 8: *Burial in Baptism*

The story is told of a picture-perfect couple. They married with great love that lasted. Their greatest hope was to have a child, to love and hold, and continue in their godly ways. Yet, there were difficulties. And since they were very faithful, they prayed unceasingly. Finally, the wife conceived, and nine months later, a little boy came crying into the world. They named him James. He was full of life, gulping down glasses of Kool-Aid, living each day as if it were his last, and dreaming through the nights.

He grew in maturity and ability until it was time to go to the church and learn the Word of God. The night before his Sunday school class, his parents sat James down and told him how important listening and understanding God's Word was. They stressed that, without the knowledge of the Bible, James would be a faded leaf taken away by the wind. He listened, wide-eyed. Yet the next day, he never arrived at the class. Instead, he found himself in the woods, swimming in the lake and climbing the trees. When he came home that night, the news of his wrongdoing had spread throughout the small church.

His parents were beside themselves, not knowing what to do. So they called in the behavior modification experts to modify James' behavior. Nevertheless, the next day he found himself in the woods, swimming in the lake and climbing the trees. So they called in the counselor, who sought to break James' "rebellious" spirit. Nevertheless, he found himself the next day, swimming in the lake and climbing the trees.

His parents grieved over their beloved son. There seemed to be no hope. At this same time, a traveling Preacher visited the church, and the parents said, "Ah! Perhaps the Preacher!" So they took James to the Preacher and told him their struggles. The Preacher replied, "Leave the boy with me, and I will have a talk with him." It was bad enough that James would not go to the church. But to leave their son alone with this godly man was terrifying. However, they had come this far, so they left him one morning at a nearby lake with the Preacher.

Now James stood on the fishing pier, and the Preacher stood in his boat. He motioned, "Come here." Trembling, James came forward. And then the Preacher picked him up, held him silently against his heart, and extended a fishing rod.

His parents came to get James, and they took him home. The next day, he went to the church to learn the Word of God. And when he finished, he went to the woods. And the Word of God became expressed with the sway of the trees, which James understood. And he swam in the lake. And the Word of God became felt in the softness of the lake, which James delighted in. And he climbed the trees. And the trees' rustling spoke the Word of God, which became the words James said.

And James grew up to become a great man. People who were afflicted by depression came to him and found joy. People who were without friends came to him and found fellowship. People with no exits came to him and found a way out. And when they came to him, he said, "I first learned the Word of God when the Preacher held me silently against His heart."[1]

The heart is traditionally understood as the seat of the soul from which strong emotions like love and rebellion arise. But the heart is not limited to the realm of emotions but includes self-will. King David had this in mind when he prayed, "Create in me a clean heart, O God, and renew a right spirit within me" (Psalm 51:10). It's what God the Father meant when He spoke, "I will put my law within them, and I will write it on their hearts" (Jeremiah 31:33). And what Jesus meant when He shared, "Blessed are the pure in heart, for they shall see God" (Matthew 5:8). As Manning suggests, "The heart is the symbol to capture the deepest essence of personhood. It symbolizes what lies at the core of our beings; it defines irreducibly who we really are."[2] It's why God, as Father—a personal being—has concerned Himself with the heart throughout history rather than behavior modification.

It's too easy for us to believe that Christianity begins with what we do for God. The tendency is to start to live by the laws—the "dos and don'ts"—we learned. To those who only focus on behavior modifications, God answers:

> *this people draw near with their mouth and honor me with their lips, while their hearts are far from me, and their fear of me is a commandment taught by men... Ah, you who hide deep from the Lord your counsel, whose deeds are in the dark...* (Isaiah 29:13, 15).

Jesus rebukes the heart of the hypocrite with "Woe to you... For you are like whitewashed tombs, which outwardly appear beautiful, but within are full of dead people's bones and all uncleanness" (Matthew 23:27).

Christianity isn't mainly concerned with the outward form but with an inward change. Success in the Christian life isn't based on how many behavioral changes occur or new habits, but a true shift in the heart—repentance. Repentance is from the Greek root word *metanoia*, meaning "a change of mind" or "a transformative change of heart." When we're devoted to heart change, we need to understand that we're constantly in the process of breaking out of the layers of our old nature and changing into the new (an attitude change that leads to a change in behavior).

Change doesn't come through adopting a set of rules that we enforce upon ourselves. For many people, repentance is the idea of a hermit living in a cave on bread and water or beating oneself with a whip trying to make right the wrongs. For others, it's the image of the Old Testament prophets who repented for their nation in burlap and ashes. Repentance is often thought of as something reserved for those who commit the most heinous of sins, an action needed "for those who have sinned more than I have." Such thoughts are grounds for repentance according to human nature.

But our journey home is very far from that. It doesn't start with someone telling you that you were a sinner and being given a list of dos and don'ts. Instead, it's a small voice on the inside that calls you homeward. It urges you to choose repentance, saying, "You aren't to be doing what you have any longer. Stop continuing in the person who you've been." Heeding that voice as the prodigal did, we choose the path of repentance, the way of transformation. God's voice to each of us speaks of not giving into fleshly motives, attitudes, and actions. His still, small voice speaks of a constant attitude of repentance.

Our journey home to the Father is marked by our change of heart towards sin. Minimizing our sin only keeps us away from Him, and we stay within the "pigpen." In repentance, the prodigal more or less said, "I have done wrong. There's nothing redeemable about it. I deserve what's coming to me. I deserve death." Upon that reflection, he was repentant, "I will never be deserving of all that is good, so I shall go back to depend on my father where I can be full." His change of attitude, or change of heart, marked his journey home—his repentance.

9 Limping Home

Figure 9: *Athlete Derek Redmond Limping Home With Father*

> *I will arise and go to my father, and I will say to him, "Father, I have sinned against heaven and before you. I am no longer worthy to be called your son. Treat me as one of your hired servants."*
>
> — **Luke 15:18-19**

We can imagine the confusion that comes with returning to the person you've disappointed—"Will I be accepted? What can I say or do to be accepted?" The prodigal son "admits that he was unable to make it on his own" and confesses that he would be better off in his father's home, "but he is still far from trusting his father's love."[1]

Preparing Speeches

No one would return home after disrespecting and rejecting their family to the extent that the son did, expecting everything to be normal as if they left for the store for fruit and returned. It's why the son's contemplation of approaching home looks like a speech. He prepares an address because he expects his father to respond the way he would respond to himself. He would be mad. "What do you want? Are you coming home to rob me more? If you don't have the money you took, get off my farm!"

In anticipation of facing his father, the son prepares an eloquent speech. If not, he expected he wouldn't even get on pop's property without being on the wrong side of a gun. So, he prepares.

It's a speech similar to the one we would give God when we start our way back to Him—if you feel you've been away from Him. Here's the message he prepares.... listen to this: "Father, I have sinned against heaven and before you. I am no longer worthy of being called your son. Treat me as one of your hired servants."

Have you ever been involved in intense discussions with absent partners, preparing for their questions with edited responses? What emotional energy we spend! We ruminate like a cow chewing its cud over and over again. We're anxious. What kind of speeches have you prepared? Explanations? Apologies? How about defenses? What about boasting or begging? Coming home is fatiguing if you still believe you can't be made worthy of love and acceptance.

Desiring Slavery

We find the son coming home still thinking he can't be a son anymore because he hasn't done right. So he figures he can return home as a hired hand—he wants relief in servanthood. The Greek word translated "hired servants" within verse nineteen refers to "day laborers." Day laborers in the first century held a much lower status than a slave. Slaves were often compensated with living quarters, clothing, etc. Life-long slaves would often be entrusted to manage business affairs and projects (see Matthew 25:14-25). Slaves could be educated, cultured, and highly skilled in an occupation. Therefore, slaves weren't necessarily of low status in that day and age.

In contrast, day laborers were desperately poor, having no one looking out for their best interest. They lived alone, often homeless. Often skill-less, the most menial or undesirable work was for them. There were no opportunities on or off the job site for a higher social or economic position. You would most likely do seasonal work. Being what day laborers were, they would be in no position to negotiate. One's interests, goals, and well-being weren't relevant in the hiring process. In Israel, one would get paid a determined wage after each day to make sure you had what you needed to survive till the next day (see Leviticus 19:13). However, in a distant land outside Israel, a hired hand's wage was not standardized, nor was it made in scheduled payments, often leading to great need, as the prodigal experienced.

In reflection of the culture, the prodigal's desire to be a hired hand seems therefore reasonable and desirable. Going home meant he would get paid regularly and be stuffed full by the generosity and compassion of the father. The desired job meant a pay increase and a great deal of stability compared to working as a hired hand of a pig farmer who paid you when he felt like it. In heading home, the prodigal shows himself to be an opportunist. His relationships are gone, and death is close. Survival is the only motive. Going for a reliable source of means with an even-tempered boss seems fitting and desirable. In a performance-based world, miserable jobs with horrific bosses are a dime a dozen. That's the harsh reality of life in the real world.[2] But where values like compassion imbue the job as something more than a job, that's special. The pleasure-seeking lifestyle isn't any match to values like compassion, generosity, and kindness.

The prodigal's solution to return as a hired hand, however, seems familiar. It's another version of his solution to be treated as one of the pigs to receive food. This was once the reality of my heart too. Honestly, I'd much rather leave God for what I believe will satisfy me, then return to Him as a servant so I can work for some substance and eat at His table, yet not have to be with Him. I can continue to feel good in my work, in what I do for God, but won't surrender to the truth that I am nothing. When my nothingness confronts me, I can simply run away to the distant land again. It takes much faith in the Father's compassion to accept that vulnerability is the way to receive healing and redemption. Nouwen describes this struggle:

> *Receiving forgiveness requires a total willingness to let God be God and do all the healing, restoring, and renewing. As long as I want to do even a part of that myself, I end up with partial solutions, such as becoming a hired servant. As a hired servant, I can still keep my distance. Still able to revolt, reject, strike, run away, or complain about my pay. As the beloved son, I have to claim my full dignity and prepare myself to become like the father.*[3]

Have Faith In Love

Coming home often feels like adding to my shame and worry. On my journey, I scheme how to receive God's forgiveness, but in reality, I only believe that I can't receive His forgiveness. Could it be that there's a God with love so scandalous, expansive, deep, vast, high, welcoming, and inclusive as to accept me in my sorry state?

The fear of rejection will make us reject grace, for to receive grace, we must have faith in the one who gives it. Fearing rejection is the self-imposed limit to our faith. We see ourselves incapable of being fearful of people who may reject us, yet we cling to fear in our hearts. Low self-esteem continues our slavery to fear. Even in loving relationships, we may have felt abandoned in a time of need. Fear of not receiving what we desire becomes a guide in all of our interactions. This type of relationship does not have perfect love.

1 John 4:18 states, "There is no fear in love, but perfect love casts out fear. For fear has to do with punishment, and whoever fears has not been perfected in love." In a way, fear of rejection and the uncertainty of the acceptance received leads to a kind of betrayal of the one who gave it. Fearing those who love us is, at best, mistrust of the person who cares. It's what happens when someone compliments you on your artwork or appearance. You immediately discuss its imperfections and follow up with comments on how they would't find it acceptable if they knew better.

Sadly, the fear of rejection leads to a kind of betrayal of all that's good—even God's presence. It would seem that we'd rather live in the cold, dark, despairing places than approach the warm light of acceptance. In a time of threat, we hide our faces that would otherwise reflect the warmth of our Savior's love.

Our temptation is to stop in our journey home in grief that we don't have the love we should for the Father. We're scared of punishment or any scorn that would widen the crack in the center of our beings, in the deep belief we are worthless and despicable. So we hide. It's self-preservation, the strong instinct of the flesh. To save us from this instinct, the prophet Isaiah writes, "a bruised reed he will not break, and a faintly burning wick he will not quench…" (Isaiah 42:3). Jesus, knowing your brokenness, will never break your spirit, never hurt you. Jesus isn't some human capable of kicking you when you're already down. In Matthew 9:36, Jesus called for intercessory prayer because "When he saw the crowds, he had compassion for them, because they were harassed and helpless, like sheep without a shepherd."

If this is indeed Jesus, He seems to become more familiar to me in my times of brokenness. Jesus becomes someone I might enjoy the presence of, and He would want mine. I don't think He will hurt me or even turn on me. But I am unsure. Disbelief lingers.

Our Greatest Challenge: Believing The Gospel Of Grace

In light of the fear of rejection which keeps us from receiving the compassion of God, the greatest challenge of the spiritual life is not perseverance in suffering, nor is it your discipline, devotion, or focus. But it's in believing the gospel of grace.

After spending sixteen months in nursing home ministry with those with disabilities in Missouri, I concluded that the greatest challenge is not any physical situation or handicap itself. The more significant challenge was in the accompanying feeling of being useless, unappreciated, unloved. As odd as it sounds, it's easier to embrace not being able to walk, dress, or feed oneself than it is to embrace not being valued by another. I've seen people in the war-torn country of South Sudan suffer immense tragedy, yet somehow begin to thrive in life. However, when there's a sense that we no longer belong, we lose our grip on life quickly.

If losing our grip on life is sensing that we no longer have anything to offer anyone, it's not surprising to know that 322 million people in the world—about the population of the United States—suffer from Depression (pre-COVID-19 era).[4] Surely, life must have a more significant meaning than staying useful in relationships and doing something! Given how the biggest obstacle in life is shame which cripples us from receiving God's grace, Jesus created the story of *The Prodigal Son* to make the statement that we should believe

God's grace to be always greater than our inabilities.

Even though he desires slavery, the prodigal makes the right choice for prayer. He meditates on coming home as a servant to his father. Although his desires are misplaced, and his true identity is not embraced, the son's recital shows his yearning to be united with his father. The recital looks a lot like prayer. Jeffrey D. Imbach, in *The Recovery of Love*, wrote, "Prayer is essentially the expression of our heart longing for love. It is not so much the listing of our requests but the breathing of our one deepest request, to be united with God as fully as possible."[5]

Our brokenness must be embraced and not scorned in our quest to choose sonship over slavery—life over death. Arriving at this state is, as Welch described, "Nakedness without shame. To be known without feeling exposed. To live without any need for self-protection."[6] Authentic human beings live out of the center of who God created them to be, knowing that they are imperfect, a mess, hypocritical, and needy, yet aren't compelled to cover it with boasts. They own no closet from which to grab an imposter to wear and parade around. Boasting is only a tool of the ignorant fool who, in his folly, thinks that shame is covered externally with an astonishing press release or flattering magazine cover. Every honorable person I have met is one who not only acknowledged but embraced the totality of the person they are, faults and weakness included. Perhaps this is why Apostle Paul shared his struggle with weakness in prayer with us:

> *So to keep me from becoming conceited because of the surpassing greatness of the revelations, a thorn was given me in the flesh, a messenger of Satan to harass*

me, to keep me from becoming conceited. Three times I pleaded with the Lord about this, that it should leave me. But he said to me, "My grace is sufficient for you, for my power is made perfect in weakness." Therefore I will boast all the more gladly of my weaknesses so that the power of Christ may rest upon me. For the sake of Christ, then, I am content with weaknesses, insults, hardships, persecutions, and calamities. For when I am weak, then I am strong (2 Corinthians 12:7-10).

In reflection of Paul's prayer and the painful prayers of my own, I have chosen to entitle the spiritual reality of the Christian life as "Limping Home." Like the prodigal, I believe we all struggle to make it home as sons and daughters. Shame has gripped us and has torn pieces out of our soul as we give bits of ourselves to it in fear. We're weak, and our nothingness cripples us. If a journey home is a choice to live as a beloved son and daughter, along the way, our nothingness will challenge us. Not only this, but insults, hardships, persecutions, and calamities will question our identity as beloved by breathing into us insecurity that curses us. Many have left the belief in their beloved-ness because they fall victim to caustic feelings. They believe they can't come home without being whole, strong, and without a wayward desire within them. Many confuse their struggle with having weaknesses as their loss of nerve and try to return, seeing God as a master who cracks the whip. They still hold the image of God as a harsh taskmaster. If we treat ourselves as indentured slaves, God will naturally become a slave driver to us in our mind, demanding and punishing. No wonder many are resentful and lose their way home. But it's the Christian who limps home regardless of shame's ravages in their body. They hear the voices which claim their un-worthlessness and may believe them for a time, but, ultimately, they have more faith in God's love.

To return home in weakness, we must come to know that grace is always greater! (We'll talk about this in chapter eleven.)

Self Hatred

We must be careful not to desire slavery when we feel self-hatred in our season of brokenness. Manning tells us that "Self-Hatred is an indecent luxury that no disciple of Jesus can afford, because self-hatred suddenly reestablishes me as the center of focus, and biblically that is idolatry."[7] Bowing down to self-hatred, and sulking in humiliation, is just another form of idolatry in the distant land. Do you believe that you must earn your position as a child of God? Do you desire the closeness of the Father but through a list of dos? Should we continue to struggle away? *Well, maybe if I perform well, I'll be good enough for the Father's embrace!* Are you afraid that you'll become fired—in a literal sense—from our Father's service?

If so, we're in a state of fear which Apostle Paul told us was of the spirit of slavery. In his letters to Timothy and the Christians in Rome, Paul writes:

> *For God gave us a spirit, not of fear but power and love and self-control. Therefore do not be ashamed of the testimony about our Lord...but share in suffering for the gospel by the power of God, who saved us and called us to a holy calling, not because of our works but because of his purpose and grace, which he gave us in Christ Jesus before the ages began* (2 Timothy 1:7-9).

> *For you did not receive the spirit of slavery to fall back into fear, but you have received the Spirit of adoption as sons, by whom we cry, "Abba! Father!"* (Romans 8:15)

God doesn't abandon those who stay at home with Him. Do you believe it? Remember, God is a father. If we based our love for our children on their performance, they wouldn't have a chance, would they? If our love is unconditional, how much more is our Heavenly Father's love! As Paul states, children of God don't live in a spirit of fear because their acceptance is not based on them or what they did. (We'll revisit this in chapters 10, 13, 17, 18, and 20.)

10 Merit Is Overrated

Figure 10: *The Tender Embrace of Forgiveness*

And he arose and came to his father. But while he was still a long way off, his father saw him and felt compassion, and ran and embraced him and kissed him. And the son said to him, "Father, I have sinned against heaven and before you. I am no longer worthy to be called your son."

— **Luke 15:20-21**

Jesus' audience understood how much the young prodigal was in a pickle without any way of escape. To be sure, the crowd's interest is piqued by the prodigal's change of heart and his hope of being received as a day laborer. There's no question for the prodigal on whether or not he should return home. It's the obvious choice. Only how to go about it is not so obvious. Will his preparation be enough to approach his father successfully? If so, what will the son have to do to stay home as a hired hand? At this point of the story, both groups are leaning in. They're like children when their teacher reads from a picture book. Both groups have more in common now than any other time: they hope to find the son's redemption and assume it would lie in a lifetime of hard labor.[1]

Challenging The Obsession With Do

Like the most devout Pharisee or the most broken sinner, we, too, come to the text with questions: "Is there redemption for the son? If so, how does the son make himself presentable? I hope there's a list… is there a list? I want to jot it down." To be sure, for life to be found for this son, it would surely be by crawling back home as a beggar to sacrifice everything for the rest of his life. A life of doing is the only choice. Everyone knows it, and everyone agrees. Both groups are obsessed with doing.

As Jesus was telling the story, on one side, you have tax-collectors and sinners who felt that they never did anything right and didn't know where they stood regarding their acceptability. They identified with the prodigal's dilemma—deep in sin, discouraged, longing for a breakthrough, longing for meaning; hoping that they could rise above messy situations. Would the prodigal find help or become more hopeless? Could he be a hired hand and survive?

On the flip side, some listened as Pharisees—those who were obsessed with good performance. Although they would have written off the son entirely as unacceptable, as they did with the tax collectors, they would've been curious to see if there was forgiveness. And, if so, what hard labor would he need to earn it? The doctrine of the Pharisees was based on achieving the wage of divine approval, not necessarily turning away from sin to face God in repentance.

At this point, the son's approach to the father is significant because the father's reaction to it is a matter of life or death. Although we find the son approaching his father, it's not the way we expect nor the way the son has rehearsed. "But while he was still a long way off, his father saw him and felt compassion, and ran and embraced him and kissed him." If I were in the crowd with Jesus, I would've interrupted Him at this point. "How could the father feel compassion when he hadn't heard the boy's story yet? Doesn't he have to hear the boy's apology and intent before feeling compassion?" Instead, the father ran to the son with compassion even before the son got to him. How scandalous of the father! We may even say the father is reckless.

Now, remember Jesus' parable (along with two previous ones he told in this setting) had mainly been in response to the scribes and Pharisees who grumbled about Him being with sinners. The story is for them to understand.

The shameful actions of the son prevented even the worst Pharisee from showing the prodigal an ounce of empathy. They built their whole lives and careers on doing the right thing, at the right time, every time. Although they were hypocritical, they were careful to maintain decency in the public eye. Even an expression of repentance in daily life or for a son to come home after rejecting his father would be an occasion for scorn. In fact, in that culture, a repentant son would be met by his father's community—confronting him, punishing him, making him wait at the city gate for days, and spitting upon him—making him a public spectacle of the father's shame (see Deuteronomy 21:18-21).

There was nothing theological or even cultural that allowed the son to be met with compassion for the scribes and Pharisees. It was out of their framework—absent in their system of reckoning. The most tender thing a rebellious son could have received would have been in being formally approached by the father, like in a cold business deal, and given terms of employment—no negotiation—in front of the townspeople. You're offered a job, but you're still an outcast from the family, their slaves, and the community (see Deuteronomy 28:15-20).

Life Beyond Do

In every parable, something represents God, and something else represents us. I can only imagine the crowd around Jesus chatting softly among themselves. The sinners in Jesus' audience are going, "I know who the father is… that's God. Surely I could be the prodigal, but there's no way God would love me like that." The doers don't know who they are yet, but they know they can't be the prodigal because, in their eyes, they're good. "In no way would God be the father because God wouldn't have compassion on a heathen" (cf. Luke 18:9).

The father embracing the son in absolute unconditional compassion reminds me of the truth found in Romans 5:8: "but God shows his love for us in that while we were still sinners, Christ died for us." Has it ever crossed your mind that when God looks at you, He would feel compassion? Has it ever occurred to you that on your deepest, darkest day, that day when that bad habit had a hold on you, or you had a fight with your spouse, or overreacted towards your son, or did something dishonest, on that day, what would happen if you asked, "I wonder what God thinks about me now?" Would it ever cross your mind that God looked at the humbled you and felt compassion?

If you are like me and all who I know, the answer is no. We don't believe the Father is compassionate because we don't understand our Heavenly Father. Maybe we have been wrong about the love of God. And this is what's at the center of what Jesus wants to teach us. Here's a father whose son insulted him so severely that he couldn't have done anything more to make the story worse. But when he saw his son, he felt compassion.

God is portrayed here as a father who refuses that we make it home by ourselves. There's no expectation for us to beg for forgiveness in the promise to do better. God here isn't a father who schemes to make it difficult for us to reach Him. Nor does He allow us to become shamed in the process of coming home. No, God leaves heaven, ignoring His dignity by running toward us, paying no heed to promises of slavery, and brings us to the table richly prepared for us.[2] God has always been the one looking out for our return, and we are the only ones who have hidden our faces from Him. What good news—God is not distant! He's not to be avoided. God is moved by our pains and meets us where we are on the road of life. He's Emmanuel—"God with us." He's a father committed to living with us to share in our sufferings as well as our joys. He loves without caution or regret. No matter how much like the pigsty we smell, He can't stop hugging us.

The father likely ran to meet his son to reach him before anyone in the community had a chance to confront, abuse, and shame him as is the cultural norm. Not only does the father spare him the humiliation of having to sit outside the city gate for several days, but he throws out the custom of making the repugnant rebel bow low and kiss his feet. No, the father humbles himself, receiving the shame that was reserved for the son. The father's behavior is undignified, wasteful, and reckless (at least in the eyes of the world).

The Way Of Wounds: Choosing *With* Rather Than *Do*

So far, the father's display of unbridled emotion towards the son is the most unbelievable feature in Jesus' story. Some of us find the idea even repulsive. But, if we dig deeper, there's a subtle truth that teaches us to accept the father's radical love, and by it, God's crazy love for us too.

The prodigal finds himself caught in a display of unbridled

emotion. Trying to regain equilibrium in the father's outrageous response, he recites his speech created while in the pigpen. He's worked so hard on it, and he feels that he must give it. So, while the father gives him a big bear hug, the son recites part of his speech. Now, speeches or apologies usually come before a warm embrace, so I can only imagine the son's speech would be the equivalent of "Wait. Not yet! My speech! You have to let me share it first. Then you can decide if I need to go to rehab or not, how long I plan to be here, and how long will it take to repay you."

But on second thought, we see the not-so-obvious detail that the son has omitted half of his speech. He now surrenders to the father's embrace, and he begins to accept his broken state—his wounds—telling his father how he sinned against him without the second half of his speech. There's no promise to do something to deserve his father's compassion. It suggests that the son has come to his father with wounds exposed—presenting his nothingness—in trust that the father will heal them without the onus to do the healing himself.

Isn't it true that when God's presence feels distant, our powerlessness seems too frightening? The darkness of feeling not truly embraced in our entirety within the world seems to affirm our un-lovableness. But when we surrender to God's embrace, fully accepting our powerlessness, admitting we can't render healing on our own, something changes for us. No longer do we desire to self-harm, receive punishment, or a life of slavery. Instead, our appreciation for tenderness becomes realized. That's all we want and need. We're comfortable with wounds because of the healing in their exposure to the one who cares. It's the gift of being vulnerable. "Vulnerable" is a word derived from Latin, which means "the way of wounds." To be vulnerable in the context of coming home is to have the courage to embrace your brokenness the way God does. It's a gift from God. Vulnerability is the only way to healing.

We find the beautiful gift of vulnerability extended to Adam and Eve by God in Genesis 3. Up until then, "God's relationship with the man and woman has not been as a casual bystander, but rather his presence is necessary for them to experience the joy they have presumably known," writes Curt Thompson, MD, in his book *The Soul of Shame*.[3] Since humankind is made in the image of a communal God,* they lived in communion with God and their fellow humans. But this state starts to slip as Adam's and Eve's shame piles up relational chaos, having eaten of the forbidden fruit which God warned against:

> *...the Lord God commanded the man, saying, "You may surely eat of every tree of the garden, but of the tree of the knowledge of good and evil you shall not eat, for in the day that you eat of it you shall surely die"* (Genesis 2:16-17).

> *So when the woman saw that the tree was good for food, and that it was a delight to the eyes, and that the tree was to be desired to make one wise, she took of its fruit and ate, and she also gave some to her husband who was with her, and he ate. Then the eyes of both were opened, and they knew that they were naked...*

---

* "Let us make man in our image" in Genesis 1:26 reveals how God lives in community within Himself—the Godhead—with the Son and Spirit.

And they sewed fig leaves together and made themselves loincloths. And they heard the sound of the Lord God walking in the garden in the cool of the day, and the man and his wife hid themselves from the presence of the Lord God among the trees of the garden. But the Lord God called to the man and said to him, "Where are you?" And he said, "I heard the sound of you in the garden, and I was afraid, because I was naked, and I hid myself." He said, "Who told you that you were naked? Have you eaten of the tree of which I commanded you not to eat?" (Genesis 3:6-11).

God had every right to withdraw His presence from Adam and Eve after their rebellion against Him. Imagine the feeling of rejection God could have experienced. Regardless of the heartbreaking situation, God comes near to them, looking for them as He's walking—calling out to them. God's not geographically challenged, nor does He lack knowledge of the whereabouts of Adam and Eve; yet He calls out to them, "Where are you?" What could this mean? As Thompson explains, "God is inquiring of the couple's internal, not their external, whereabouts."[4] He's deeply concerned and invested in their spiritual lives, relational health, and emotional well-being. Throughout the biblical narrative, God shows Himself to be a father who cares for us even when we have abandoned Him. He doesn't hide from us when we hide from Him. God's the one who pursues, comes near, and finds us. Contrary to our thoughts, God doesn't walk away from us, nor does He leave us out of mind.[5]

Remarkably, God asks a question to Adam and Eve, "Where are you?" He doesn't state a demand or threat like a human would with knowledge of a loved one's betrayal. There's nothing in the text suggesting that God is questioning them in an accusatory manner: "Aha, I know what you've done, and now you have hell to pay!"[6] No, when God comes, He comes with questions. "He is the one pursuing answers," trying to find you to be with you.[7] In His question, God moves towards them, actively creating space for them to encounter their inner state of brokenness. Providing an opportunity for them to choose to be with Him in their broken condition.

God's question, "Where are you?" shows us that we should use vulnerability in the moment of shame. It's almost as if God is saying, "Come out of hiding! It's safe to be with me." It's not an invitation to get hurt, be exposed, or an opportunity to inflict them with the emotions He's experiencing. As Thompson suggests, "He is looking for us because he longs for us to be with him even as he is with us, for us to know his delight with us which is present at all times, even in the midst of other things he may simultaneously feel."[8]

Upon reflection on the parable of *The Prodigal Son*, we can assume that God is walking with speed in the Garden of Eden, with urgency. He's calling out with a deep longing to connect with the couple. Like the father of the prodigal, the Father in the Garden of Eden is compassionately gifting His wayward children with vulnerability—the space where wounds are exposed and healed simultaneously.

God's welcoming presence and the gift of vulnerability drew out His people. It was a moment of choosing for rather than against a relationship with Him. In the face of shame, Adam admits that (1) he hid because (2) he was afraid (3) and he was naked (verse ten). Adam is acting courageously here. Shame instructs us that vulnerability—the way of wounds—doesn't lead to healing but potential abandonment. It's why humanity hides from God in the beginning. Fear naturally follows shame as shame instructs us to anticipate the abandonment that is coming to us.

We'll only learn to embrace our complete self, although broken in its many pieces, by growing in the awareness of God's desire for our total selves—wounds and all. It isn't enough to say prayers several times a day and occasionally give Him our attention. We can't live for God some days and not others. It's not enough to be grateful for His goodness yet move on from there to pursue our agenda. It's no good to present the presentable parts of our lives to God yet reserve the rest for "our eyes only." We can't come into His healing presence without showing all our wounds—there's no returning to God with just half of our being.

Suppose you feel resistance to being fully embraced by God; could it be an unacknowledged desire for enslavement? Slavery would allow us to keep our distance without having to trust in God's gift of sonship. You and I had rather be free to come and go from home as a slave working for our value than be a child who's utterly dependent on their father for value. The truth is that only when we surrender ourselves entirely to God's healing presence by passing through the state of vulnerability can we expect to be healed from our wounds and have a real connection with God and others again. To be healed, you've got to be real. There's no other way.

Tragedy radically alters your direction in life, but it's the vulnerability we experience there which allows us to receive the power of Christ in His present risen-ness that we wouldn't share with Him at another time.[9]

Do you dare to place your brokenness under the blessing of God, not taking on the attitude of a slave demanding to do the healing yourself? We can't accept grace until we embrace our wretchedness in God's presence. Love never starts with what we do for God, but what He does for us. The spirit of sonship is not about doing—that's the mark of slavery—but about being with the Father. We'll discuss this further in chapter fourteen, but in the meantime, let's discuss the father's response to the prodigal son's abridged speech.

11 Grace Is Always Greater

Figure 11: *The Return*

But the father said to his servants, "Bring quickly the best robe, and put it on him, and put a ring on his hand, and shoes on his feet. And bring the fattened calf and kill it, and let us eat and celebrate. For this my son was dead, and is alive again; he was lost, and is found..."

— **Luke 15:22-24**

We need to understand the weight of the above scripture passage. It's like your neighbors having a son named Jimmy. He's been in and out of rehab for drugs. And he one day broke into his parent's house, stealing everything. He disappears for two years. And all of a sudden, you receive a call from his parents, "You know Jimmy, right?"

"Yeah, heartbreak Jimmy," you reply.

"Well, he just showed up on the driveway, and we are going to have a party today!"

You and I would be skeptical at best: "It's a little early for a party. Is he back for you or just out to steal from you again? What about his rehab? Does he have a job? Has he changed? And is it a heartfelt change?"

These are routine questions. You would get similar questions coming from a potential employer of an ex-convict. But the parents are saying, "I don't care about anything right now. My son is home!"

Jesus is making a not-so-subtle point to the doers in the audience: the boy had done nothing whatsoever to earn acceptance. I bet all the religious folk went, "So, what happened to the need to put things in their proper order?" The entire system of the Old Testament is for priests and sacrifices, among other things, to please God. But their theology lacked grace—that sinners who missed the mark could stand accepted before the Father without a lifetime of work and flawless performance. Jesus has shattered what they understood to be the standard protocol. Grace is greater than do or what's left undone. As MacArthur reveals:

> *They had even enshrined their own intricate system of finely detailed traditions as the chief means by which they thought it possible to acquire the kind of merit they believed would balance out the guilt of sin. That is why they were obsessed with ostentatious works, religious rituals, spiritual stunts, ceremonial displays of righteousness, and other external and cosmetic achievements. And they clung doggedly to that system...*[1]

The parable debunks the false idea that performance is the key to justify your existence. Your return to the Father, submitting to His authority and love over you, is enough (see Genesis 15:6 and Romans 4). Such a belief is hard to adopt in the face of past experiences. We must fight the voice that tells us the future is only the past revisited, and we must endure it.[2] The successful spiritual life is not in how much "grime" you can clean off of yourself or your ability to save yourself from a fall that would otherwise be embarrassing. Neither is it hiding all we know and feel about ourselves behind some appearance or approach that we hope will be more pleasing. The successful spiritual life looks like a prodigal limping home, scarred, bruised, broken, arriving because he wants to be home.

So the party gets started here in the story. And to be sure, the youngest son feels awkward and confused. He would still be trying to say, "I don't deserve a party. I'll need to work hard and well first." But, regardless of any protest, gifts are brought out. We'll talk about the significance of these gifts later in chapter thirteen. For now, know they point to the bestowal of all rights, privileges, and honors of a son, with all their legal weight.

We must remember how God's grace triumphs over all "not-having-done" or marks missed in life. Standing in the world, we crave satisfaction. If we turn to the substance of God's presence and glory, His life-giving grace will satisfy our deepest needs and longings. Come to God not complete, not prepared, not clean, and not presentable, but broken, unclean, and hungry. God is glorified when we hunger and thirst in Him alone (see Psalm 63:1). For this reason, we have cause for celebration.

A Journal Entry: Preparing Speeches

Preparing speeches is what I do best. It's what I've been educated and trained to do. But there's nothing that prepared me to craft a speech to give to a crowd of people directly affected by my suicide attempt.

I walked through the doors of the church Sunday. Not a lot of people would look at me. No one approached me, shook my hand, or embraced me. I felt ashamed. The few notes I got up to speak with were from my Bible studies when I was in the hospital. After explaining why I attempted suicide, I asked for forgiveness. Most accepted my apology. I was glad to have been embraced afterward with hugs and tears. However, there were a few that refused to look at me and left the meeting quickly.

I went to social media that week to explain my actions because the news was out. But, unfortunately, my post went without a lot of responses. What really hurt was a lady posting on social media how I deserved no dignity and how the church shouldn't have taken care of me during my crisis. Even a long-time friend commented that I ought never to return to ministry, that I was broken goods, a man of weak character.

It was one week from my attempt, and I hadn't given it much thought to talking with God about my attempt until then. I was putting it off, thinking I would be shunned and shamed if I were to ask for forgiveness. But I talked with Him, starting with an apology, and went on to give my explanation with a promise to do better. Something happened, though. It seemed like it wasn't appropriate to provide an explanation or guarantees—just my return to Him in my change of heart was enough. I felt that God told me how He wanted to mourn with me over the past several weeks and the years that led up to my attempt. He wanted to mourn with me for all the lost times, looking for love but receiving rejection. He wanted to share in my disappointments for all the times I was away from Him when He wanted so badly for me to be home with Him.

I waved my arms in the air—I was giving up trying to hold my emotions back. Until then, I attempted to cover up my feelings and hide thoughts that I thought weren't acceptable. But it was here that I began to let loose. I cried. I shared how I was broken by life, my dreams were shattered, and how harsh the world is without an ounce of compassion. I even told God I was angry at Him but didn't want to be and how I had hatred for those who had hurt me. There wasn't the feeling that God demanded the right feelings since I was laying them before Him to heal. I ended with how I did wrong, leaving His presence, not trusting in His best for me.

His hand resting on me reassured me. "It's alright, now. You're with me now. The world will crush you, but I never will. You've been lost, and I have been looking for you. I've found you again. Come home; be with me. The winter has gone, green growth have appeared in the land, the time for pruning and singing has come. The time has come for you to learn how to be a son whom I love."

My life's mission is now about coming home—reuniting with myself, God, and those who love me with the grace of God—and learning to live again as a beloved son.

12 Getting Over Yourself

Figure 12: *Peter Alerted*

But the father said to his servants, "Bring quickly the best robe, and put it on him, and put a ring on his hand, and shoes on his feet. And bring the fattened calf and kill it, and let us eat and celebrate. For this my son was dead, and is alive again; he was lost, and is found." And they began to celebrate.

— **Luke 15:22-24**

I like to think that once the prodigal son became surrounded by everyone celebrating his homecoming, he'd struggled to identify with the person everyone in the house was treating him as. To be sure, the prodigal felt awkward. He would still be trying to say, "I don't deserve a party. I'll need to work hard and well first." But whatever he dealt with must have been resolved at some point because everyone began to celebrate together. Thus, the son's sonship is reclaimed, despite not working for it.

Here lies the mystery of the Christian's spiritual life. Our actual guilt and shame that stands before a brazen heaven "can be removed only upon the basis of the finished work of Christ plus nothing on our part."[1] In his book *True Spirituality*, Francis Schaeffer tells us:

> *The Bible's whole emphasis is that there must be no humanistic note added at any point in the accepting of the gospel. It is the infinite value of the finished work of Christ... upon the cross plus nothing that is the sole*

basis for the removal of our guilt. When we thus come, believing God, the Bible says we are declared justified by God, the guilt is gone, and we are returned to fellowship with God—the very thing for which we were created in the first place.[2]

The event of accepting the finished work of Christ to purify us is just that. The Bible tells us that our faith is not placed in "faith" as an abstract entity or force but the actual person and work of Christ. Neither is it faith in self or belief in love—that's new-age thinking. It's not Kierkegaard's concept of faith—a mere jump into the dark. Faith isn't a belief in a solution but trust in the already realized Solution. Faith is hope made real, believing the specific, concrete promises of God. It's accepting that God alone has the answers and the solution. As Schaeffer describes faith, it's "believing the specific promises of God; no longer turning our backs on them, no longer calling God a liar, but raising the empty hands of faith and accepting that finished work of Christ as it was fulfilled in history upon the cross."[3] The very moment we pass from death to life, from the kingdom of darkness to the kingdom of God, we become embraced as children of God.[4] This only happens through a spiritual rebirth, which occurs in the event of baptism (see Romans 6:4).

Just as physical life begins through physical birth, spiritual life begins through spiritual birth. There's no other way to start the Christian life. Jesus Christ said to an inquiring Pharisee, Nicodemus, that if this rebirth doesn't occur, we can't enter the kingdom of God. "Unless one is born of water and the Spirit, he cannot enter the kingdom of God. That which is born of the flesh is flesh, and that which is born of the Spirit is spirit" (John 3:5-6). Christ continues in discussion with Nicodemus, telling him that whoever believes in Him may have eternal life and not perish.

Later, Apostle Peter instructed on the occasion of this rebirth and new life. When crowds were told of the good news on the day of Pentecost, how they had killed the Christ but God raised Him into newness of life for them, they were cut to the heart and asked, "Brothers, what shall we do?" (Acts 2:37). And Peter said to them:

> *"Repent and be baptized every one of you in the name of Jesus Christ for the forgiveness of your sins, and you will receive the gift of the Holy Spirit. For the promise is for you and for your children and for all who are far off, everyone whom the Lord our God calls to himself."* And with many other words, he bore witness and continued to encourage them, saying, *"Save yourselves from this crooked generation."* So those who received his word were baptized... (Acts 2:38-41a).

Water baptism (immersion) is the occasion in which we identify with Christ and become identified with His pure life and works. Nothing more needs to be done. You're new.

Don't Despise Your Brokenness

I notice a reluctance to reveal my nothingness and embrace my new identity in Christ whenever I don't love God as He truly is. Our deflective default is to make ourselves clean. If we see ourselves as able to scrub up, make amends, and fix what we broke, we're only minimizing our problem.[5] There's grave danger for those who minimize their broken state as fixable by themselves, as shown by the prodigal's first choice of working in a pig pen as a slave. If we try to cleanse ourselves, we have more confidence in our efforts than in the loving mercy of God, who can never be contaminated. This attitude is idolatry. You make God out to be a liar—He can't do what He wants to do with you. It's why some folks never come home. They profess faith but deny it with their lives.

Welch explains, "If you live as though that forgiveness needs a small boost from your grief or good works, then you don't understand what he did."[6] Our human concepts of gospel and God can prevent us from fully embracing the gospel.[7] In our distortions of who God is to us, having hope in God merely means enduring the wretchedness of our souls. To us, there's no reason to celebrate. The only solution is "endure to the end," coming to church, worshiping, going home to lives of quiet desperation. We're just one of the faces in the crowd, another worm in the bucket. What deception! As Meister Eckhart encourages, "Pray that [we] may be quit of [our image of God] to find God."

Because we love our children, we correct, instruct, and even discipline them to grow up as the adults they should be. But we're not stern taskmasters (I hope). I would suggest that God is the same with His children, but even better. So, don't limit God or put Him in chains devised by your conception of Him. If you make Him too small or too far away to help, that's self-pity, and you'll never merit His help. He's greater than your imagination and experience.

When I was going through intense hurt after the breakup with my fiancée, my fear of rejection became much more intense. I was overwhelmed with the fear of rejection when thinking of my girlfriend telling me she had never really given her whole heart to me throughout the relationship. The fear was keeping me away from our compassionate God.

One night I was too uncomfortable to sleep. So I listened to music. Although I can't usually enjoy modern Christian music—which I regard as "prom music"—I listened to Steffany Gretzinger of Bethel Music sing "Pieces." The song says that God doesn't give His love in pieces, nor is He disengaged. That truth hit me like a falling anvil. God's love and care aren't like any other love I had known. It isn't the fickle, half-hearted, cautious love I learned from my girlfriend. It's not love handed out in installments based on how pleasing you are. Nor is His care the "care" I received from the psychologist who threw a phone at me for not pronouncing the names of my medications correctly. God's love and care are uniquely His own. His love keeps its promises, regardless of my ability to keep my own. Such love is unbelievable in comparison to the love the world gives. It's why I believe that the greatest challenge of the spiritual life isn't perseverance in suffering, nor is it our discipline, devotion, or focus. It's in believing the gospel of grace.

The Bible presents such a different picture of children of God than what most of us have. There's unrelenting compassion for you which dresses you in resplendent attire (see chapter fourteen). But there's a great divorce between our hearts and heads, which somehow endured our spiritual birth. Of this state, Manning shares his experience:

> *It used to be that I never felt safe with myself unless I was performing flawlessly. My desire to be perfect had transcended my desire for God. Tyrannized by an all-or-nothing mentality, I interpreted weakness as mediocrity and inconsistency as a loss of nerve. I dismissed compassion and self-acceptance as inappropriate responses. My jaded perception of*

personal failure and inadequacy led to a loss of self-esteem, triggering episodes of mild depression and heavy anxiety.[8]

Even having walked with Jesus, knowing Him intimately, being face-to-face with Him, we may still believe that we aren't worthy of the title of "son," "daughter," or "friend"—those titles are reserved for someone else like Noah or Moses. To be about the Lord's business, intimately aware of His whereabouts and His glorious work, is often pushed away in our unhealthy reflection of our weaknesses and inconsistencies—we say there's a loss of nerve. We become a "lost cause."

Peter Represents Us

We see Apostle Peter's struggle with identity after he fails to own up as a follower of Jesus on the night He was detained:

Then they seized him [Jesus] and led him away, bringing him into the high priest's house, and Peter was following at a distance. And when they had kindled a fire in the middle of the courtyard and sat down together, Peter sat down among them. Then a servant girl, seeing him as he sat in the light and looking closely at him, said, "This man also was with him." But he denied it, saying, "Woman, I do not know him" (Luke 22:54-57).

Jesus was tried before the high priests, which eventually led to His wrongful conviction under the cover of night. Peter was watching Him while He was detained. He was careful not to get too close, lest he became identified as a student of Jesus. Coming close that night to warm himself, the flames of a charcoal fire lit his face, exposing his noticeable Galilean features (see John 18:18). Once his true identity was questioned—an identity everyone condemned—Peter denied Jesus, swearing he never knew his Rabbi, having no relationship with His Father.

But Jesus had already predicted that Peter would fail Him that night: "before the rooster crows, you will deny me three times" (Matthew 26:34). Being the loyal, courageous person he was, Peter contests Jesus' prediction by protesting how he was incapable of such an act of treason. He goes as far as to say that he's the last person that Jesus should suspect as disloyal. "Even if all fall away on account of you, I never will" (Matthew 26:33 NIV). Remembering what he told Jesus that night, he goes out to weep uncontrollably after his third denial.

As a man who has just denied his best friend, Peter would have naturally felt that he wasn't able to carry on the mission of Christ. Peter didn't just make any mistake; he made an utterly shameful one. Even though Jesus had shared how he would be given the keys to the kingdom, I'm sure Peter thought that nothing stood true. Maybe Peter felt as we do—our inconsistency is proof that we don't care about God. The evidence of this attitude in Peter is revealed by his going back to fish, back to his old occupation and identity—what he was strong in and comfortable with.

Like the day before he met Jesus, there's a night where Peter didn't catch anything (see Luke 5:5 and John 21). Perhaps this made him recall his need for Jesus in life. To be sure, he was frustrated. Maybe he cried, "I can't do anything good without Jesus. And I can't be with Jesus because I'm a bad disciple."

When daylight came, Peter traveled back to shore to call it quits. When he wasn't too far away from the beach, he saw a man standing on the shore calling out to him. The voice commanded him to cast his nets on the right-hand side of the boat with the promise of catching something. Peter had nothing to lose in that moment; he'd already lost Jesus, or should I say, he was already lost.

After swinging his nets over to the right, a catch so big as to break the nets came in. John, who was with Peter, realized, "It is the Lord! It's Jesus!" (Jesus, when he first met Peter, called out to him to cast his net to receive a catch. So this event would have jogged his memory and the emotions attached to it [see Luke 5:1-11].) In his excitement, Peter dived into the lake and swam 300 feet to where Jesus stood. When Peter got to land, something strange happened:

> When they got out on land, they saw a charcoal fire with fish laid out on it and bread. Jesus said to them, "Bring some of the fish that you have just caught." So Simon Peter went aboard and hauled the net ashore, full of large fish, 153 of them. And although there were so many, the net was not torn. Jesus said to them, "Come and have breakfast." Now, none of the disciples dared ask him, "Who are you?" They knew it was the Lord. Jesus came and took the bread and gave it to them, and so with the fish. This was now the third time that Jesus was revealed to the disciples after being raised from the dead. When they had finished breakfast, Jesus said to Simon Peter, "Simon, son of John, do you love me more than these?" He said to him, "Yes, Lord; you know that I love you." He said to him, "Feed my lambs." He said to him a second time, "Simon, son of John, do

> *you love me?" He said to him, "Yes, Lord; you know that I love you." He said to him, "Tend my sheep." He said to him the third time, "Simon, son of John, do you love me?" Peter was grieved because he said to him the third time, "Do you love me?" and he said to him, "Lord, you know everything; you know that I love you." Jesus said to him, "Feed my sheep"* (John 21:9-17).

It would have been a confusing occasion for Peter. Jesus is alive; that's wonderful. But Jesus is the one he had just refused his loyalty to. If there were an awkward silence, it would have broken when Jesus said to Peter, "Come and have breakfast." Grabbing breakfast together is something that intimate friends do. Maybe Peter's guilt and shame started to wane while eating, but to be sure, he became paralyzed when he saw that Jesus was cooking breakfast on a charcoal fire. Like the one on the night that Peter warmed his hands over, and he failed Jesus. Shame, to be sure, was triggered. And to make matters more traumatically shameful, Jesus broke bread and gave it to Peter, just like the night Peter told Jesus that he would never be disloyal. No dialogue is apparent during this sharing of bread and fish—only uncomfortable silence. I would've eaten my breakfast slowly that morning if I were Peter.

After finishing, Jesus looks at Peter and asks, "Simon Peter, son of Jonah, do you love Me more than these?" OK. Jesus was using the full name of Peter. This isn't easy. Only a mother would use a full name, and it's when things go wrong. For Peter, his full name included his old name, "Simon." Of course, Peter would have expected Jesus to regard him as an unchanged man—he resuscitated his old self. What Peter wouldn't have anticipated was that Jesus asked if he loved Him more than these. Jesus is referring to those sad words of Peter before the other disciples shortly before denying Him: "Though they all fall away because of you, I will never fall away." Right then and there, Peter would have vividly felt the real sense of his failure.

    Now Jesus doesn't intend on making this reference to shame Peter, but to reveal Peter's powerlessness to himself and for him to receive grace. Jesus' question of whether or not Peter loves Him is to rid Peter of any confidence he has in himself. Thus, Jesus gives Peter another chance at being reliant on His power.

    What's astonishing about Jesus' question is what kind of love He chooses to ask for. The word used for love here is *agapaō* (ἀγαπάω), meaning agape, the highest form of love. Agape refers to the choice of one person out of many. It often implies that you regard someone as satisfaction among all else. Peter answers, "Yes, you know I *phileō* you." Such a natural response! Phileō (φιλέω) is brotherly love—of which the American city of Philadelphia is named. Peter tells of a friendship kind of love that exists between him and Jesus. He adds not, "more than these," but prefixes an appeal to Jesus' all-knowingness of Peter's incomplete love.

    Peter's response isn't an insult, but a response made in complete awareness of how Jesus loves him and he, himself, lacks the spine to love Jesus the same way. Peter's telling Jesus, "You're God. You know that I don't love you to the highest degree. I am unable to return to you the unconditional love you have for me. But yet we share friendship."

    Jesus asks again, "Peter, but do you love me?" The need for the repetitive question is for Peter's wounds to become reopened.

Answering the same way as before, Peter repeats his nothingness. "Jesus, I really have nothing else to offer you!" All of the imposters, false identities and vain self-confidence in the flesh are acknowledged and nullified in Peter's persistence.

Jesus repeats His question yet again, but this time He asks, "Peter, do you love Me like a brother?" This time Jesus uses the same word used by Peter, phileo, for love. He has come down to Peter's level of relating. Peter becomes grieved. Maybe it's the third go at the question that reminds Peter of his third denial of Jesus. Perhaps for the first time, Peter feels his utter nothingness before Jesus, the one with the perfect love. He has nothing to offer Jesus, the Son of God, but mere human affection. But maybe, too, Peter is painfully aware that Jesus is reaching out to him, drawing him in again with His way of loving, not making demands but simply accepting him.

Jesus, as the skilled Physician, is preparing Peter's broken heart to receive the good news again. Peter didn't need a bandage covering his nothingness but a new heart to fill his vast void. What no one expects is for Jesus, this third time, to have asked for brotherly love instead of the highest form of love, agape. Jesus is making a point: "Peter, you can't ever love the way I love you. I'll meet you in your desire for friendship. You can't do what I have done, so I'll meet you where you are. The only requirement to be with me in a loving relationship is to desire friendship with me and know there is no other way." This new honesty of Peter's availed the opportunity for Jesus to identify with Peter and for Peter to identify with Jesus. They become brothers in this event, with God being their Father (cf. Hebrews 2:11). Peter finds acceptance and becomes reinstated as an Apostle of Christ.

Like Peter, we must respond to Jesus with what type of love we have for Him. The love we have will reveal who God is to us. Our honesty will admit that we do not love Jesus with the highest form of love most of the time. At best, we often love Jesus as a friend.

I want to be clear: the Bible is clear that the ultimate essence of evil is the failure to be the most satisfied in God; that we are to love Him with all our heart, mind, and soul—our whole being (see Matthew 22:37). If God isn't our highest satisfaction, there isn't an establishment of a meaningful relationship with the Father. However, I believe that the human will is weak, and to confess before God that we don't have the highest love for Him is a state of repentance, where we trust God to lead us into a more profound love for Him. This doesn't mean Jesus becomes to us like a drinking buddy. But, I do believe it means Jesus and the Father become our highest satisfaction when relying on His love for us and not our love for Him. And what's the love of that between a father and child? How about a love that is non-transactional? Yes. And this is why, if we hope to match God's love for us, we will always short-circuit the plans God has for us because we will never be God.

"What kind of love do I love God with?" is the biggest question we must always keep on asking. We should choose to love God as the one who loves us without condition, regret, or caution. He is our Father. His absolute choice of you was displayed on the cross—choosing to die in place of you. God would rather die than be without you. And God only asks that we stop, be surprised, stand in utter amazement, in what Manning describes as "letting your mouth hang open, gasping in absolute astonishment." Walk with Jesus—befriend Him.

It was hearts that had become hardened towards Him that Jesus condemned, not those who knew they were broken, weak, with nothing to offer. We must remember how God's grace triumphs over all "not-having-done" or missing the mark in life. If we tell God we can be to Him what He is to us, other than a friend, we deny Him of who He must be to us—our all-powerful, all-loving Father.

When I realize who I am, the totality of my needs and inabilities, the natural choice is to let God be my Father and for Jesus to be my Deliverer and friend, which I couldn't be for myself. If I make anything out of the fact that I am Thomas Kilian, I am dead. And, if I make anything out of the fact that I am in charge of the pigpen, I am dead.[9] So, how can we embrace Jesus as a friend?

Thomas Merton says it's in quitting "keeping score all together and surrender ourselves with all our sinfulness to God who sees neither the score nor the scorekeeper but only his child redeemed by Christ."[10] Julian of Norwich seized this truth with stunning simplicity when she wrote:

> *Some of us believe that God is almighty and can do everything; and that he is all-wise and may do everything; but that he is all-love and will do everything—there we drawback. As I see it, this ignorance is the greatest of all hindrances to God's lovers.*[11]

If we fail to have faith—concrete hope—in God as our Father, thinking He's only a father to the Billy Grahams or Mother Teresas of this world, we, in essence, kill the proper image of God on the altar of emotions. It's why Apostle Paul tells us, "For it is shameful even to speak of the things that they do in secret. But when anything is exposed by the light, it becomes visible, for anything that becomes visible is light..." (Ephesians 5:12-14a). As Manning ponders:

> *God not only forgives and forgets our shameful deeds but even turns their darkness into light... Christians who remain in hiding continue to live a lie. We deny the reality of our sin... If we conceal our wounds out of fear and shame, our inner darkness can neither be illuminated nor become a light for others.*[12]

We often beat ourselves with the past with bad feelings, not letting God heal us of our wounds. As Dietrich Bonhoeffer said, "Guilt is an idol." But when we dare to live as forgiven men and women, we join those healed and draw closer to the Father.[13] Let's embrace our brokenness, grieve over it, but not grow callous by it. Within vulnerability, we come to mourn what we have become and the loss of love experienced to allow God to be God. Let the Healer be the healer. Only then will we hear music and dancing, a cause for celebration. In such moments, we aren't a spectator but a participant —the prodigal son limping home.[14]

A Journal Entry: The Right Love To Love With

I'm having a hard time choosing the right love to love God with. There are few moments in which I'm genuinely most satisfied in God. I'm disappointed that I don't have the love I should for God. I'm always choosing against God, leaving home. Afterward, I come home to choose God. When I am away, famished for belonging and fulfillment, His grace and goodness at home seem so satisfying in those moments. I am troubled by returning home, only to leave again.

I think of God's creation work and Adam and Eve in the Garden of Eden. After each day of creation, it's recorded that God declared His work as being good. But have I ever wondered why He called it good? After all, this passage doesn't appear to be a discourse on ethics.

While God declared all works as good, man, the last of creation, was announced as existing very good. Perhaps I need to know that creation was made for us as a good gift, fitting our needs. So, Adam and Eve indulging in the forbidden fruit of the tree of the knowledge of good and evil, takes on a whole new meaning. We were given good gifts out of God's pure grace, lacking nothing. Even so, we expressed through eating the forbidden fruit that we thought we knew ourselves and our needs better than God. Thus, we chose our "gifts" against the good gifts of God.

My sin goes beyond the refusal of God's good gifts in the decision to gift myself with what I think is good. As a result, my rationale is flawed, and my intellect is damaged.

I lack trust in God's choices of good for me. I'm frustrated because what I call good seems so satisfying in the moment, although I know that God's choices must be the most satisfying. I am therefore rejecting God and rejecting true fulfillment.

I'd much rather leave God for what I believe will satisfy me, then return to Him as a slave so I can work for some sustenance and eat at His table, yet don't have to be with Him. Then, I can continue to feel good in my work, in what I do for God, but I don't have to surrender to the truth that I am nothing.

This is the reality of my heart. I must reveal this to God, asking to transform me by His grace in spending time in prayer, asking that His riches of grace in His presence will be most satisfying to me. Just spending time with Him has allowed me to have the right love. He has become my highest satisfaction.

13 Life At Home

Figure 13: *Home, Solace From The Desert*

But the father said to his servants, "Bring quickly the best robe, and put it on him, and put a ring on his hand, and shoes on his feet. And bring the fattened calf and kill it, and let us eat and celebrate. For this my son was dead, and is alive again; he was lost, and is found."

And they began to celebrate.

— **Luke 15:22-24**

Home is the inner sanctuary, the center of our being, where we can hear the voice that says: "You are my beloved, with whom I am well pleased." It's the voice that announced from heaven that Jesus, after His baptism, was the beloved Son of God on whom blessedness now rested (see Matthew 3:16-17). It's the life-giving voice that spoke Adam into existence and continued to speak to him in the Garden of Eden in the cool of the day (see Genesis chapters 1-3).

Just the sound of that voice tells us that we're home with nothing to fear: no fear of giving yourself and then being rejected, no fear of having to prove yourself to receive a gift. You can receive acclamation without parading it around as proof of your goodness. You can accept without feeling indebted, give without the expectation of receiving anything in return. You may do great things and help many people without the need for affirmation. As the beloved, you can suffer great tragedy and receive the cruelest of treatments from humankind without ever having to doubt the love that is freely given you by your Father.[1]

Home is living in awareness of the divine relationship, the attention to my true self within Christ as His beloved. This understanding follows that leaving home is when we no longer believe with radical trust that blessing and life always have and will always rest on our shoulders as the beloved when we are with God the Father.

The imagery in the return home of the young son in Luke 15:22-24 is a beautiful depiction of being at home. Home is a place of celebration for the newness of life. After facing his father in repentance, the prodigal son receives a party. The father orders his servants to quickly prepare a banquet as if the wayward son is a dignitary to be honored—with gifts, celebration, and the formal bestowal of high privileges.

- Sandals—given to the son as a symbolic statement, announcing him as accepted and crowned as son and estate master.

- The robe—an elaborate artisan-crafted coat (the equivalent of the twenty-first-century tailored tuxedo)—made him like a nobleman or a groom at his wedding. Given the Greek expression here in verse 22, "first-ranking garment," the son is outfitted like an army general or a CEO. (This is reminiscent of Joseph's ornate robe gifted by his father in Genesis 37.)

- The ring—a symbol of authority with the family crest or seal: when pressed into wax on a formal document, the ring's seal served as legal authentication.

All the gifts point to absolute rights, privileges, and honors being bestowed with all legal authority on the wasteful son as if he earned them on his own.* What the father owns is now the son's too (cf. Ephesians 3:20).

To describe this bestowal spiritually on the sons and daughters of God, Apostle Paul writes in Romans 4:5 that Christ "justifies the ungodly." To be justified means to be counted and declared as good. Meaning we are made legitimate offspring in the sight of the Father.

We Receive Honor

The father's plan of regaining the son's presence is a picture of God's mystery now revealed by and in Christ. Conceiving His redemption plan before time began, God determined that, in Christ, people would be gathered to Him by their faith. Since God's intention is always kind, He found it desirable to reveal the mystery of His choice to those who believe. Those who believe in Him and depend on His works are His legitimate children. (After all, how could the good gifts that the Father desires to bestow upon His creation ever be experienced as good while in a cloud of disbelief? [cf. Romans 8:28]) This privilege isn't because of anything we do or will do—for He purposed our choosing before we came into existence—before we could do anything (see Ephesians 1:1-14).

Just as the father is delighted to bestow the son with special privileges, although the son did nothing to earn them, so it is with

---

* This concept is accurately expressed in the Vulgate by the Latin phrase *Usufruct*, meaning "use of the fruits." It describes the legal right to use someone else's assets without limitation and reap the proceeds of its harvest as if they were one's own.

the Children of God. God's disciples aren't selected because of merit but simply because God loves and continues to love His creation. Love is found in His goodness, and there's nothing that makes us earn God's love (see Ephesians 2:10).

In the ancient world, if someone is adopted, that person receives the family name and inheritance with full rights and responsibilities.[2] Paul's use of the term adoption (*husiothesia* in the Greek or "the making of a son") in his letter to the Romans is central to our interpretation of the prodigal's experience. Adoption, as a legal term, always includes the context of slavery—slaves always had the potential to become adopted as official household members if the master so chose.[3] The Roman ceremony of adoption speaks primarily of the liberation of a minor from servanthood to adoption.

In every sense of the term, adoption into sonship marks the climax of Jesus' parable and expresses our redemption provided by God the Father. Dr. William Hendrikson explains, "Redemption implies emancipation from the curse, that is, from the guilt, punishment, and power of sin (see John 8:34; Romans 7:14) and restoration to true liberty (see John 8:36; Galatians 5:1)."[4] Redemption implies the freeing and the release from slavery.* Disciples have been delivered from the slavery of sin by the payment of a ransom or debt. The means of our liberation is Christ's sacrificial blood (see 1 Peter 1:19; Isaiah 53:10; 2 Corinthians 5:21).

It's Christ's sacrifice on the cross that gives us the opportunity for deliverance (see Ephesians 2:8). This is why redemption and forgiveness are closely linked in our study of the relationship we have

---

* *apolytrōsis* is the Greek verb used in Scripture for redemption, meaning "release."

with God. Forgiveness is the remission of sin or the "removal of sins" —because our debt has been paid. Christians have not only been brought back to God but also stand cleansed from all sin. God's decree in Jeremiah 31:34, "For I will forgive their iniquity, and I will remember their sin no more," is a prime example of forgiveness as the removal of sins.

Jesus' use of adoption within the parable draws partly from Hellenistic law and the elaborate Roman ceremony. Adoption in Hellenistic rule is an institution connected with a considerable emphasis on inheritance.[5] Galatians 4:5 speaks of the adoption attitude which marks believers heirs. Those adopted by God don't receive a slave mentality but the mind of a son of the house. The concept of the slave being freed as a son in the act of adoption is found in Romans 8:15.*

The homecoming celebration and ceremony of sonship in Luke 15 is a vivid picture of this occasion. Like the son receiving all the lavish riches, we're told in Ephesians 1:8 that God lavishes gifts on us—those who have believed—because of His grace. As the son received a signet ring to show his identity, Paul tells us that we have received a seal or authentication of our sonship by the gift of the Holy Spirit (see Ephesians 1:13). Disciples are marked as God's possession by the Holy Spirit, who validates a disciple's inheritance and sonship (see Ephesians 1:14; 2 Timothy 2:19). Disciples are given the Holy Spirit as a "token or proof that they… belong to God."[6]

---

* In Greek, Romans 8:15 tells us that the Spirit whom the convert receives, works as πνεῦμα υἱοΘεσίας (the son of the house) as opposed to δουλείας (such a spirit is possessed by a slave).

We now understand the meaning of the gifts bestowed on us as displayed in the reception of the prodigal son. We've been chosen for greatness as disciples as the Father sets us apart. So we should decide to share the purpose of His kingdom and seek separateness onto it. We've inherited holy responsibilities as adopted sons and daughters, which means we must act in life as saints.

Sainthood

Other than sonship, the concept of sainthood is best at conveying life at home with the Father. Without it, being at home is vague, presumptuous, and can even be disastrous. Leon Bloy's words, from his book *The Woman Who Was Poor*, have the taste of such truth: "The only real sadness, the only real failure, the only great tragedy in life, is not to become a saint."[7]

When the term "sainthood" is mentioned, particular images, figures, and methods often come to mind. Unfortunately, they do us a disservice. Saints are often depicted as White and sometimes "rich individuals who dedicated their lives to enshrining themselves in non-white cultures."[8] Such men and women are praised for their work of "saving" people, yet their obsession for "charity" influences their cause more than their desire to help ever had.[9] Many are like Mother Teresa, who told the suffering and needy that they were being "kissed by Jesus" and discouraged the use of western medicine, yet "spent lavish sums on her own medical treatments."[10] Sainthood might be synonymous with hypocrisy—false righteousness equal to bold wickedness; however, the true concept of sainthood is the opposite of this. True sainthood is reserved for those who caution against self-righteousness and a claim of superior wisdom and goodness. Saints are weak men and women who ignore the poor pitiful puny things they sometimes manage to do for God in recognition that they're nothing without Him.

Apostle Paul is one such saint who sums up his Christian life as considering "everything as loss because of the surpassing worth of knowing Christ Jesus my Lord. For his sake, I have suffered the loss of all things and count them as rubbish [excrement],* in order that I may gain Christ" (Philippians 3:8). These words echo those of Prophet Isaiah, "We have all become like one who is unclean, and all our righteous deeds are like a polluted garment [soiled menstrual pad].* We all fade like a leaf, and our iniquities, like the wind, take us away" (Isaiah 64:6).

True saints are men and women who know they're flawed with throbbing weaknesses and character defects. They are those who learn that brokenness is the human condition but don't let their nothingness keep them from the Father. It's the daily, active pursuit of repentance—facing the Father, revealing our unlovable, inconsistent, irritable ways, and turning to Him to be loved and forgiven. Saints dare to live as the forgiven. As Manning says, saints move on from unworthiness to "advance in love which has redeemed and renewed [them]… in God's likeness."[11] Afterward, they laugh at having lived away from the Father in shame.

The call to be unified with the Father isn't just given to the devoted Christian who overcomes every bad habit and never misses

---

* The Greek word σκύβαλον used here is translated as "dung."
* The Hebrew words עִדָּה and בֶּגֶד used here is a phrase translated as "menstruation covering."

church on Sunday. Neither is it reserved for those who travel to foreign places to evangelize or for those who obtain doctorates in Bible and theology. Paraphrasing Jean Vanier, it's not reserved for the well-deserving or those who do courageous things, but for people living ordinary lives with needs.[12] It's those who hunger and thirst for all that's good to be perfected. It includes those who beg for another day, another chance, people with broken hearts who live apart from the world's ways, those who care about making amends, and those who flee from their enemies to find safety.

Saints are you and me who are holy because we belong to God.

14 Tailor-Made

Figure 14: *High Priest In Holied Garments*

> *But the father said to his servants,*
> *"Bring quickly the best robe, and put it on him..."*
>
> **— Luke 15:22**

At the start of the WWE-like smack-down scene in the movie, *The Peanut Butter Falcon*, Zack, a man with down syndrome played by Zack Gottsagen, bursts through barns doors, presenting himself to the crowds. Then, with arms raised, he declares victory—prematurely. "He's wearing a freakin cardboard box." Nothing was even intelligible, and the Sharpie'd "PBF" added to the vagueness. But that didn't matter. He wanted to be a professional wrestler and wanted to play the part. And while he was miles from TV cameras, at that moment, confidently standing in his homemade costume, the young man became, in his mind, everything he had dreamed of being.

Have you ever felt more attractive, exotic, or more human when wearing something you liked? Clothes exist in two categories, ordinary clothes and beautifying clothes. Common clothes are for daily life, for clean and rough activities. Beautifying clothes, such as formal clothing, are set apart for social occasions. When worn, we're identified with respectable things such as attractiveness, sincerity, respectability, and mental well-being. When wearing everyday clothes, you're ordinary. Heck, you might find a vagrant bum wearing the same shirt as you. But when you wear beautifying clothes, there seems to be something extraordinary about your identity.

I remember when I was four years old, seeing a man dressed in a lime-green suit. "That's a nice suit!" I yelled. I'd never seen a lime-green suit, so I assumed that the bright color signified something special. From that day onward, I loved wearing suits. In university, people knew me to "overdress." Some paid attention to me when previously they didn't. Formal clothing made me stand up straight; when wearing sweats, I was hunched over. I noticed my response to myself and my identity was completely different depending on what I wore. Maybe this is why it's often said, "The makeover will start with clothes."

For the young prodigal, the gift of new clothes started his makeover—a mark of a new identity. It's why the nakedness of the prodigal son is met with his father's response: "Bring quickly the best robe, and put it on him." He received a tailored robe, which covered his thin body, replacing his beggar rags. Rembrandt's depiction of the prodigal son leaves us with no doubt about his condition. He no longer has long curly hair; he is shaven like a prisoner of a concentration camp or war, robbed of one of the marks of his individuality. His weak skeletal frame has no outerwear but a yellowish-brown undergarment that's tattered because of its exposure to harsh elements. He has nothing covering his frail body. Nothing covers his nakedness and shame.

If we know anything, we'd know that the prodigal's state is similar to ours. Just as he made himself naked and ashamed, so have we. Like Adam and Eve, we hide, not wanting to be seen, with leaves never large enough to cover our nakedness. So, in compassion, God's first response was to clothe us with animal skins (see Genesis 3:21).

There's a powerful message here. There's good news in being covered because it's better to be dressed than found naked. But it was certainly not the most favorable attire since the covering was of dead animals—a message that marked its wearers as unclean. "You don't have to be a vegan to imagine how such clothes were a bit gross," says Welch.[1] Although such clothing reeked of death, blood, and sacrifice, it was better than being bare.

The second time God provided clothing to humans, the clothes had a very different purpose. In contrast to the animal skins worn by Adam and Eve, the new garments given were attractive and beautiful.[2] Everyone agreed… they looked spectacular. What's so special about these garments is how they were or set apart by God for Himself. And those who wore them became set apart too:

> *Then bring near to you Aaron your brother, and his sons with him, from among the people of Israel, to serve me as priests—Aaron and Aaron's sons, Nadab and Abihu, Eleazar and Ithamar. And you shall make holy [sanctified] garments for Aaron your brother, for glory and for beauty. You shall speak to all the skillful, whom I have filled with a spirit of skill, that they make Aaron's garments to consecrate [set apart] him for my priesthood… holy garments… shall receive gold, blue and purple and scarlet yarns, and fine twined linen… stones, and engrave on them, as a jeweler engraves signets, with the names of the sons of Israel… make settings of gold filigree, and two chains of pure gold, twisted like cords; and you shall attach the corded chains to the settings* (Exodus 28:1-3; 5; 9; 13-14).

This passage only details one piece of the garment, the ephod (the sleeveless garment). But there are five more pieces to the elaborate costume: an embroidered coat, a waistband, undergarments, and a hat. Although there are lengthy tailoring instructions for each, their point stands out: This is an extraordinary and spectacular garment because they belong to God. It's no "lime-green suit," and it's most certainly not a coat made from a dead goat. It's way better!

The key phrases to discover here are "sanctify" and "to consecrate." The term sanctify (sometimes expressed as holy) is the state of being separated from all defilement. The phrase to consecrate describes the state of being set apart, meaning to make and set aside something for a divine purpose and use. We know what this means when we take an everyday item that, after it's cleaned, we set aside for special use. It's like washing an expensive platter and stowing it away for the next celebration. So, for an item or person to be sanctified meant that the common could be made clean and be set apart for greatness. That's great news. The average, ordinary person can be made new, cleansed from their stains of sin, and reserved for God's glorious works.

Much of the Old Testament makes essential distinctions about clean and unclean things, the common and the sanctified. The differences enumerated are endless and detailed. This matter of clean and dirty may not seem highly relevant to our lives, but if we give pause, we'll see something familiar to us.[3] Welch alerts us:

> *Since the common contains both the clean and the unclean, we can simplify it this way. The universe exists in three categories: unclean, clean, and holy. Our goal is*

to get clean, stay clean, and then set our sights on the holy. The holy can be intimidating, but only when we enter that realm can we have true fellowship with God. Whether we know it or not, this is what we truly want. We aim to be holy and enjoy the presence of the Holy One. That is the deepest answer to the problem of shame.[4]

What if I told you that there was a misunderstanding you just had while reading about Aaron and his sons? Something you may have missed was how they were chosen as priests because of God's mere choice. They were ordinary Joes before putting on the sanctified garments. When they wore the special robes, they were identified as priests; hence, they were given them for "their dignity and honor."[5]

The priests knew they hadn't earned that role but still knew they were priests when in their robes. Like we wear a uniform for work, knowing that we're representing a boss or business and their values, the priests knew who and what they represented while in their priestly garments. The title of priest was only a gift, borrowed while on duty, and "as a result, they were neighbors, shoppers, parents, little league coaches—regular people, until they got dressed," says Welch.[6]

The wearer of a uniform changes the status of the person. It's the point of why the tailored robe covers the prodigal. The garments associate him with his father in that the dignity and honor of the father is shared with him. It symbolizes what occurs when spiritually clothed: we become God's ambassadors with dignity and honor. His garments which clothe us announce that we belong; no longer are we outsiders—no longer do we have to live as we once did.[7]

So far, we know that ordinary people can live extraordinary lives. This splendor does occur. Imagine that! And it happens when we are clothed. Just as an extraordinary one replaced the first garment under God's old agreement with His people, there's are even more glorious garments to be worn by those under His new agreement in Christ.

The New Self

We've seen that a new identity is given through our discovery of the prodigal son's transformation. When you read the New Testament, the new attire we are clothed in is Christ Himself. In Galatians 3:27, Apostle Paul writes, "For all of you who were baptized into Christ have clothed yourselves with Christ" (NASB). There's much meaning in the term "clothed." In Greek, it's the passive state of going into a garment, meaning God, Himself, dresses us. Paul says that we've been clothed in Christ the moment we go into Christ at baptism. Going into the waters—completely immersed—isn't just a symbolic event but the occasion when we became wrapped with Christ's life and work, all of which is righteous and glorious.

Apostle Paul writes of baptism as the event in which we identify with Christ and are credited with His pure life and works. Just as Christ died and was buried, we too are baptized into His death and buried with Him in the watery grave. Paul calls this moment of being identified with Christ's work a "union" only available to those counted as dead to sin and alive to Christ. (We'll discuss this in chapter twenty.)

We're cloaked within Christ, which means we are representatives in uniform. And if we're in uniform, we're busy being about Christ's business. The text suggests that we're little Christs, His ambassadors, much like the Old Testament priests, Christians are in the world but not of it. They're sanctified onto the uncommon, that which is holy. It's why we're told to die to what is earthly in us. We have a new way of living in the world—a new way of being—and we'll see how that's such a liberating thing!

A Journal Entry: Clothed in Blessing

I was outside meditating as I walked back and forth on a plank of wood with a blanket covering me. I wrapped the blanket over my head, and it felt to me at the moment to be God's blessing on me and His love around me. His love at that moment became soft, not demanding, warm, not cold. There was something protective about it that made me feel safe from all the uncertainty of this precarious world.

The blanket that enveloped me felt to me to be God's favor clothing me. It led me to meditate on Joseph of the Bible. Father Jacob had adorned his favorite son, Joseph, with a coat that had long sleeves and different colors (see Genesis 37:3). The coat symbolized favor and royalty. People scorned Joseph out of jealousy because of it. People didn't understand how an average boy deserved to be acquainted with such splendor and status.

So, too, has my Father adorned me as His beloved. Many, too, have not understood the gift bequeathed on me. Of course, they'll hate the favor that adorns me—but it's simply that. As for me, I delight in God's blessing and wear my garment every day. My being is made secure by it. And my privilege of both sitting and walking with Christ in the heavenly realms is marked by being the wearer of such favor. Such resolve was Joseph's resolve to be the wearer of his tailored coat that eventually led him further into God's plan of placing him second in command over all of Egypt.

I'm starting to see that I will go through times of scorn because of God's tailored favor upon me, but I will be afforded rest, safety, and life by continuing to walk dressed. Too often, I have refused to wear God's favor because I believe I'm unworthy, believing the inward and outward voices that condemn me to uselessness. But I know my faith in God's favor makes me worthy in Christ.

    I'm now coming into awareness of what Johannes Metz called "the poverty of uniqueness." It's my courageous answer and a lonely yes to live out the call of Jesus, standing firm in my identity as a child of God, regardless of whether or not I have the support and encouragement of those around me. It may mean my embracing my hang-ups and personality quirks to be who I am and not necessarily who others say I ought to be. It's deciding that nothing will change the fact that I'm the beloved of God, that my mistakes and humanness do not diminish my value as God's child as long as I'm with Him. It's clinging with white knuckles to my uniqueness and even mysterious personality as God's child, no matter the scorn I face.

15 The Art of Celebration

Figure 15: *Sanctify Me*

"and let us eat and celebrate. For this my son was dead, and is alive again; he was lost, and is found." And they began to celebrate.

— Luke 15:23-24

These things I have spoken to you, that my joy may be in you, and that your joy may be full.

— John 15:11

Readers of Jesus' parable of *The Prodigal Son* often don't realize how the gifts bestowed by the father didn't initially exist for the wayward son. Such items in a typical household of that day and culture would be reserved for the first-born son and bestowed after his wedding. In the parable, this expectation is shattered. It would be no "Dad popping the cork of that 1984 Piper's Brook Cabernet Sauvignon he's been saving for a special occasion." That would be crazy. No, this event is more than crazy: It's radical. In the father's thoughts, his wayward son's return needs to be treated like a wedding—the highest of all celebrations.

Jesus Makes Wine

The wedding feast of John 2 is vital to understanding why there's a reason for celebration when the wrong and broken come home. If you were an Israelite in that day and age, your wedding celebration was a huge deal, and it would carry on for several days. It was the most significant event of your life. But in John 2, tragically, there's a disaster. The wine runs out in the middle of the feast. Shame is brought to the party. And this is what the wedding feast of John 2 is about. The text reads as follows:

> *On the third day there was a wedding at Cana in Galilee, and the mother of Jesus was there. Jesus also was invited to the wedding with his disciples. When the wine ran out, the mother of Jesus said to him, "They have no wine." And Jesus said to her, "Woman, what does this have to do with me? My hour has not yet come." His mother said to the servants, "Do whatever he tells you." Now there were six stone water jars there for the Jewish rites of purification, each holding twenty or thirty gallons. Jesus said to the servants, "Fill the jars with water." And they filled them up to the brim. And he said to them, "Now draw some out and take it to the master of the feast." So they took it. When the master of the feast tasted the water now become wine, and did not know where it came from (though the servants who had drawn the water knew), the master of the feast called the bridegroom and said to him, "Everyone serves the good wine first, and when people have drunk freely, then the poor wine. But you have kept the good wine until now." This, the first of his signs, Jesus did at Cana in Galilee, and manifested his glory. And his disciples believed in him. After this he went down to Capernaum, with his mother and his brothers and his disciples, and they stayed there for a few days (John 2:1-12).*

In John 2, we find Jesus attending a wedding reception where the wine had run out. Thus the wedding becomes the place and moment of Christ's first public exercise of divine power, turning 150 gallons of water into the best wine people ever tasted. But why wine, and wine of the best kind?

The key to this passage is near the end in verse 11. The encounter with Jesus isn't just a miracle—it's a sign. When you're a candidate for public office or a business launching a brand or campaign, you'll completely control the first presentation to make sure everything conveys the message of what you're all about. Within Jesus' first presentation, nobody is dying that needs care, no demon-possessed man is present to counsel, there are no disabled people to heal, no audience there to hear a sermon. Yet, of all the miracles He could do, making wine is Jesus' first miracle. Why would Jesus' first signifier of His mission be "to keep a party going… with great wine"?[1]

Jesus says, "I'm the Lord of the feasts. In the end, I come to bring great joy." It's why Jesus' first miracle is to make a great party. But why? Why wasn't this an already great party?

The newlyweds in John 2 have a severe issue within a shame and honor culture. The celebration they're hosting, attended by friends, family, and community, is about to fail. Someone didn't prepare. They're going to come up lacking, not having enough wine. They'll disgrace their family because everyone will assume they didn't care enough or didn't have enough money for the most significant event in their life. If the wine ran out, shame would befall them. The incredible fact is how Jesus makes wine to rescue them from that shame.

We'd have no appreciation for Jesus' solution—this absolute miracle—if we didn't understand that the newlyweds' problem reflects our sin problem. For many of us, sin and imperfections grate on us. But this outlook isn't enough to fully appreciate Jesus' solution. According to the Bible, we have impurities to be cleansed of and shame to be rescued from because we are lacking. We know this to be accurate as I believe that we know that something is wrong with us because we are trying to prove we're not of poor quality. The Rocky character in the first *Rocky* film expresses what I mean.

When Rocky is in bed with Adrian, he suddenly says, "You know, I don't really want to win the fight. I just want to go the distance."

Adrian, in bewilderment, asks, "Why?"

"If I just go the distance, then I will know that I'm not a bum." This Philadelphia-American term "bum" refers to someone of poor quality who lacks value. I would suggest that the reason we strive so hard in education, approval, status, career, etc., is that we're trying to prove to ourselves and everyone else that we're not a bum.

In *Chariots of Fire*, Harold Abrams makes a rather shocking statement about why he's driven to win the hundred-yard dash. Just before the traditional "dash" or sprint alongside one of Cambridge college's hallowed corridors, he says, "I'll raise my eyes and look down that corridor… with ten lonely seconds to justify my whole existence." He's open and honest about something that we all experience but may not want to admit. We don't only want to live well and make a contribution to society—make our mark—but also prove that we're not faulty—that we aren't a bum; wasted space.[2]

Life is to be celebrated and enjoyed but left to our own devices and poor management, life becomes a glaring stain to cover over... not celebrated. That's our problem.

Our life can be likened to the wedding feast in John 2. It's a celebration, but we have come up lacking, and the whole thing disgraces us. So, because there's something wrong with us and we couldn't fix it, Jesus steps in.

When He decides to make the water into wine, he deliberately chooses not any containers but certain vessels to accomplish His miracle. He does so by filling up the same jars used for the Jews' ceremonial washing.

Here is why this matters. Judaism, or more specifically the Old Testament, had a huge set of rites and regulations. They all pointed to how God is holy or set apart and that there's something flawed with us spiritually. To make us right, something must be done to make atonement for our sin (sin is "missing the mark"). Since God is other than what we are and people are made in His image, something must be done to make us presentable to maintain fellowship between the human and Devine. That's why purification rites came in.

If anything unclean, such as dead animals, touched anything (ex. — clothing and the body), it became unclean and need of washing (see Leviticus 11:32–40). Washing included the item or person to be soaked or bathed in a clean vessel. Stone vessels were not subject to the impurity laws in Leviticus 11:32–35, which demand that clay vessels that become unclean must be smashed. So even if stone vessels come into contact with unclean things, they remain clean. If you are concerned with purity or are in a priestly household in charge of purification duties, stone vessels would serve well as they could be reused after cleaning something unclean. Very efficient and economical. So their presence within the household in Cana indicates either that we are in a priestly household or at least a household concerned with purity. In short, this household follows the law.

For Christ to use stone vessels, purposed for pure water, to make wine, is not Jesus doing away with a "nasty," "dehumanizing" system that originated with God Himself. Why? Look at Jesus' insistence that He "has not come to do away with the law, but to fulfill it" (Matthew 5:17), and by Paul's insistence that Jesus' life and ministry "fulfilled" or was "according to the Scriptures" (see 1 Corinthians 15:3–4, John 2:6; and John 4:22).

Reading carefully, we see the story's climax isn't the contrast between water and wine—but that the best wine has been kept until last. Just as John 1:16 talks of Jesus bringing grace (the grace of the gospel) in place of grace (the grace of the law), so this miracle compares Jesus with the law as the best wine following good wine.*

The incredible fact is how Jesus rescues the newlyweds from their shame to show us that He will complete for them what they couldn't do themselves. Just like He wants to do for us. We couldn't make ourselves clean forever, as we constantly came up short under the law. He replaces the idea of using sacrifices and cleansing works,

---

* John 1:1 reads, "For from his fullness we have all received, grace in place of grace."

hinting at what He has come to do. Now Jesus comes, and life is something to be celebrated. And this is why Jesus had to make wine in cleansing vessels at a wedding and not at a funeral. He gives us new life!

Jesus wanted to keep the party going. As Timothy Keller answers, "Jesus came to bring festival joy. He is the true master of the Banquet, the Lord of the Feast."[3] Jesus is the ultimate MC. It means that being saved from our poor performance—"filthy rags" (see Isaiah 64:6; Philippians 3:4-11)—isn't only an impersonal verdict but is also a subjective and experiential event.[4] As we will see later in chapters eighteen and nineteen the cause of celebration of the prodigal's return, and the celebration occurring in our Father's home when we return to Him, becomes described by the sounds of "music and dancing" for good reason. There is sensory language about salvation throughout the whole Bible, such as in Psalm 34:8, "Taste and see that the Lord is good." Faith is a rational belief in the Father's grace, and the natural expression of this faith is celebration.

In his famous sermon "A Divine and Supernatural Light," Jonathan Edwards said:

> *There is a difference between having a belief that God is holy and gracious and having a new sense within the heart of the loveliness and beauty of that holiness and grace. The difference between believing that God is gracious and tasting that God is gracious is as different as having a rational belief that honey is sweet and having the actual sense of its sweetness.*[5]

In J.R.R. Tolkien's *Lord of the Rings*, when Samwise Gamgee wakes up from having been rescued from the fires of Mount Doom, he says to Gandalf, "I thought you were dead, then I thought I was dead. Is everything sad going to become untrue?" Jesus and the Bible tell us that He will ultimately bring this joy Gamgee speaks of. Jesus, however, doesn't just say He comes to bring ultimate joy at the end of time (see Isaiah 25:8), but also a joy to experience right here and now. Jesus is recorded as saying, "The thief comes only to steal and kill and destroy. I came that they may have life and have it abundantly" (John 10:10). It doesn't mean we won't suffer, but it does mean that we have a different sense of suffering.

In Fyodor Dostoyevsky's *The Brothers Karamazov*, a remarkable statement is made that would make sense of suffering:

> *I believe like a child that suffering will be healed and made up for, that all the humiliating absurdity of human contradictions will vanish like a pitiful mirage, like the despicable fabrication of the impotent and infinitely small Euclidian mind of man, that in the world's finale, at the moment of eternal harmony, something so precious will come to pass that it will suffice for all hearts, for the comforting of all resentments, for the atonement of all the crimes of humanity, of all the blood they've shed; that it will make it not only possible to forgive but to justify all that has happened with men...*[6]

Dostoyevsky's Christianity is showing here. Joy will be coming in the end that will make all our suffering look like a single bad day. Our current joy is nothing in comparison to the joy in the end (see Romans 8:18). But, it's still joy. Charles Spurgeon wrote of his joy as a Christian in these terms:

> *Some of us know what it is like to be too happy to live.*
> *We have so overpoweringly experienced the love of God*
> *on some occasions that we almost had to ask to stop the*
> *delight, for we could endure it no more. If God did not*
> *veil his love and glory a bit more, we would die for joy.*[7]

Not surprisingly, Jesus gives His listeners the image of celebration and feasting when talking about the wayward son's redemption in the parable of *The Prodigal Son*. Likewise, Jesus always gave His followers the impression of celebration and feasting when discussing bringing salvation to them (see Matthew 8:11). Jesus' second coming is said to be the ultimate party-feast for His followers (see Isaiah 25).[8] The phrase "on the third day" in John's narrative of the Cana wedding feast points to this as it may show us the anticipation of the day of Jesus' resurrection, the first day of the week, and the first day of the new creation produced by His dying and rising again. I see the wedding itself as presaging the eschatological wedding banquet of God with His people (see Revelation 19.7–9). Even more astounding is that He left a meal—what we today call the Lord's Supper—as a sign of His saving grace. It's therefore fitting to say that there's no other way to live a life at home with God than to live life as a celebration.

A Journal Entry: "The Beloved" Experience

Those whom I love, I reprove and discipline, so be zealous and repent. Behold, I stand at the door and knock. If anyone hears my voice and opens the door, I will come in to him and eat with him, and he with me. The one who conquers, I will grant him to sit with me on my throne, as I also conquered and sat down with my Father on his throne.

— **Revelation 3:19-21**

Jesus calls me to take part in the most intimate act of the Jew, fellowship over a meal—friendship. With a tender call, He knocks on the door of my heart. "I want to have friendship with you." He desires to come into my inner sanctuary, my heart's womb, share life-giving blessings, and experience intimate friendship with me. If I open myself to Him, I repent of the closed doors of the past. For me to say yes to the friendship of Jesus is to be a victor. He invites me to sit down with Him as a conqueror, a victor in life now and life hereafter.

"Abide in me, and I in you" (John 15:4a).

"Abide in my love" (John 15:9b).

Jesus is telling me to make my home in Him, as He makes His home in me.

No longer do I call you servants, for the servant does not know what his master is doing, but I have called you friends, for all that I have heard from my Father I have made known to you (John 15:15).

If the Christian life is not based on loving friendship, I don't think it would be possible to endure. Jesus calls us friends and a friend knows all your weaknesses but loves you all the same—even likes you. This truth is hard to trust. I guess that's why Paul Tillich wrote, "Faith is the courage to accept acceptance."

It was tough for me because I never had a strong desire for God, never a passion. I'd known for most of my life how Noah and Moses were friends of God. I'd known for a long time too how Christians are called the Bride of Christ. I always felt that it was more of a metaphor, but it eventually became known as a fact. But even when I saw it was the reality of my existence, I never felt that Jesus was my friend or husband. Maybe it's because I'm a man, and have known little about friendship; it seemed weird for me. But it wasn't until my fiancée dumped me that I gravitated towards the reality that God is my lover and friend.

I've burned with passion for my fiancée, and now she's gone. My passion for my church and all those I cared for is gone as well. The same with my friends. That connection and intimacy I felt and longed for have been thwarted. I often will not sleep at night because I'm feeling all alone and misunderstood by people. I've awakened in the night with nightmares. My body sleeps, but my heart is awake. I've allowed resentment and wounded emotions to eat me up. With a callous heart, I've walked around not letting anyone come into my heart to affect me, rejecting all relationships. I've been so focused on my work performance and art that I've felt only imprisoned—no more smiles. Everything is treated with the utmost seriousness.

But it wasn't until the day that intimacy and passion were restored to me, that I then heard a song. The Spirit led me to Song of Solomon 5: 2-6a. Passion sprang alive in me, but this time for the Father.

> *I slept, but my heart was awake.*
> *A sound! My beloved is knocking.*
> *"Open to me, my sister, my love,*
> *my dove, my perfect one,*
> *for my head is wet with dew*
> *my locks with the drops of the night."*
> *I had put off my garments*
> *how could I put it on?*
> *I had bathed my feet;*
> *how could I soil them?*
> *My beloved put his hand to the latch,*
> *and my heart was thrilled within me.*
> *I arose to open to my beloved,*
> *and my hands dripped with myrrh,*
> *my fingers with liquid myrrh,*
> *on the handles of the bolt.*
> *I opened to my beloved...*

I'm the bride who searches for her beloved.

All this time, I've heard Christ knocking on the door of my heart, trying to gain my attention. I'm half awake, with a stirring passion for the day I'll have the consolation not yet arrived. When I hear the voice of Christ, I mistake Him for an intruder or neighbor needing a favor. I don't get up to let Him in; it's too much of a hassle. But then I feel the passion that drives Him to come in, and the desire for life and all that is beautiful is made alive in me once again. Love is sparked inside me because of the love He has for me. All of a sudden, everything mundane is made beautiful. My hands become vessels blooming with life. Energy fills me.

Before, my soul failed me, mistaking Christ's presence for a stranger. Now, my soul has been enlightened by His desire for me, and He becomes familiar to me—my highest satisfaction.

I now find myself finding no shame in reaching out my hand at night, imagining taking hold of Christ's hand. I fall asleep quicker. Dreams are sweeter. And, occasionally, I'll wake myself up with spiritual songs sung by my soul. I greet Christ in the morning, telling Him how I feel instead of all the resentments I once had. I no longer need to have promises of what I can do for Him because now I just rest in the knowledge that He knows me (cf. John 13:23).

16 Doers are Party Poopers

Figure 16: *Irate*

Now his older son was in the field, and as he came and drew near to the house, he heard music and dancing. And he called one of the servants and asked what these things meant. And he said to him, "Your brother has come, and your father has killed the fattened calf, because he has received him back safe and sound." But he was angry and refused to go in. His father came out and entreated him, but he answered his father, "Look, these many years I have slaved for you, and I never disobeyed your command, yet you never gave me a young goat, that I might celebrate with my friends. But when this son of yours came, who has devoured your property with prostitutes, you killed the fattened calf for him!"

— **Luke 15:25-30**

The older son is the third character in the parable, and he's the doer who represents Jesus' main point of the story. The older son's resentment of his younger brother is apparent, mirroring the scribes' and Pharisees' blatant contempt for tax collectors and sinners. The sinners were lawbreakers who had "no interest in fulfilling someone else's expectations or demands—especially God's,"[1] while the tax collectors exploited the people for their benefit.

On the other hand, the scribes and Pharisees declared their interest in fulfilling all expectations and demands, especially God's (or what they perceived as His). They did many things in the name of God, but they had no relationship with Him. It's this attitude towards the Father that Jesus portrays in the older son. So far, Jesus has dealt at length with the prodigal son, addressing how someone without exemplary accomplishments could find wholeness. Now, Jesus focuses the spotlight on the older son, a person who seems to do everything right but never finds fullness.

Almost every reader of the parable assumes that the elder son represents a true believer because he's not rebellious but working for the home. The assumption comes as no surprise, given how the rebellious son was the one that left home for a harsh world. So, of course, the son who stayed home is the most fulfilled and freed, right? But, like everything so far, we're wrong in our assumption. As MacArthur bluntly observes, "The elder brother turns out to be just as lost and hopelessly enslaved to sin as his brother ever was."[2] In my analysis, this "do good-er" is the more enslaved and the more dissatisfied of the two.

We have to look beyond the apparent resentment of the older brother to see that the whole reality in which he lives is a lie, and he's emotionally unbalanced. By no means is he portrayed as a nice guy who has it all together, who just happens to need an attitude adjustment. Here's why. Through the older son's resentment, Jesus is revealing who this son depicts: the religious hypocrite.

The Pharisees followed the story as an outsider, having nothing to relate to until this moment. They've been casting judgment on the prodigal, the father, and even Jesus, for their conduct—after all, aren't adherence to culture and common decency what professional doers tend to enjoy doing? To be sure, throughout the story, they probably were very vocal about their disapproval of Jesus' unorthodox ways—with crossed arms and furrowed brows to boot. The real reason they're with Jesus listening to His story is that they love to be critical. Most importantly, it's a story that they expected would express the principle they devoted their lives to: those with poor performance will, in the end, be punished with the appropriate consequences. And Jesus, being the wonderful storyteller He was, entrapped them in their own game and "put them under the microscope."[3]

There are several important things to note about where the elder son takes center stage. He's "in the field," and like anyone away for work without a cellphone, he hasn't the slightest clue about the day's happenings at home. Even so, this is odd given that a huge celebration is well underway—he heard music and dancing (well beyond the beginning of a party). To be sure, those (most likely the whole community) invited had time to come home from work and get washed and dressed for the formal occasion. To be sure, the working son would have heard the news. Moreover, an elder son, especially in that age and culture, would typically have been the MC of such a party because his father would entrust that responsibility to no one else.[4] However, it's now apparent that the elder son was kept in the dark about the party. But why?

Perhaps the older son didn't have a good relationship with his father, just like his brother didn't. Maybe the father deliberately avoided having him involved. Much like the father allowed his youngest to do his own thing in a distant land, he had allowed his oldest to work out his plan in the fields. As a result, both brothers had little interest in being at home to share in their father's vision. On top of this, where was the eldest son when the youngest rebelled? Wouldn't some relationship have existed with the younger that he could have used to dissuade his brother? Nope. There's very little intimacy in the household.

Both sons are living estranged from their father—and everyone knows it. One left home, and one didn't. Both, however, lived a lie. Both chose to seek their way of gaining what they wanted—affirmation, wealth, prestige, for value and meaning in life. And both are revealed as bums. Their lifestyle excluded them from meaningfully participating in the world with fulfilling relationships. Now they've come home to two different receptions. Why? Each of them came with different attitudes or spirits. The younger went with a heart of sonship. The older went with a spirit of slavery. How do we know this to be true? Look at how the elder son protests the party.

The older son tells his father, "I've been slaving for you." What does this mean? It means he's about to give a different version of the speech his brother just delivered. The younger brother came home saying, "I haven't, I haven't, I haven't." The elder brother now is saying, "I have, I have, I have." What's more, he's saying, "I have always been obedient! I have always done right. I've been slaving away, doing everything I can. And I haven't been rewarded in the slightest!"

Notice how the older son refers to his brother as "This son of yours." What he more or less is saying is, "Dad, I hate to break it to you, but your son has taken your honest-made money and used it for hookers, and Lord knows what else! And that's what you're celebrating. You're a disgrace. You've had too much wine; you're not thinking right." It would seem like a reasonable and decent objection.

At this point in Jesus' parable, the religious leaders now know who they are in the story. They agree with the elder son. "I would feel the same way. We feel the same way about those friends of Jesus, those tax-collectors. We don't know why he loves them, why he accepts them, and especially celebrate in their home with them. These people are unlovable and wrong!" The religious leaders and the elder brother have a shared conviction: slackers should be punished, and workers should be rewarded. "There's no reason to party with sinners, and we are not going join-in either!"

At this point, we would do well to pay attention to the words of MacArthur: "The elder brother's surprise is perfectly understandable; his extreme indignation is not so easily excused."[5] This older brother isn't only a glass-half-empty kind of guy or your average suspicious legalist who dislikes cheer, but he's a protestor devoid of natural affection.[6] You would've thought that this man would've run to his dad excitedly after hearing music and dancing—cheerfully asking, "What happened, Dad? What's the good news? What are we celebrating?" If that would've happened, to be sure, the father's announcement of "Your brother is home" would be the occasion of a tear fest, a strong embrace, and filled wine glasses held high in a cheer. But, none of this happens. He doesn't even go to the father. Instead, the father has to come out to him. (Yes—the father came out to meet with both sons on his own accord).

The son remains outside, exposed to the elements, refusing to get anywhere close to the celebration, which would've gladly welcomed him. Instead, he goes to one of the servants (a preadolescent boy according to the translated Greek word "servant") outside to ask, "what do these things mean?" (these things, meaning music and dancing.) In the Greek text, this phrase Jesus uses reveals how the elder son is repeatedly demanding in an intimidating way an explanation as if the celebration was complete madness. "What is going on? How is it that I am the last to know? I didn't give my advice on this, nor the OK." For the older brother, a celebration is bad news, and the worst news is one thrown for a returning son who hasn't done anything to deserve it.

The more alarming thing is that the elder son's protest isn't so much towards his brother as it is towards his father. The father hasn't only "received him back safe and sound" (meaning the rebellious son is now literally hygienic and presentable), but there's been a killing of their grass-fed and finished calf. Killing a fatted calf in the presence of someone in that time was a clear statement of an occasion for celebration, forgiveness, and demonstration of peace. Having visited North and East Africa often, I know what this is all about. When prestigious guests arrive at our village, or we want to enter a peace agreement with a neighboring tribe concerning land division on which to graze cattle, you kill your best goat. But here, the occasion which the father says is worthy of killing the fattened calf is what the elder son sees, according to tradition, as highly inappropriate. The elder son is jealous. As far as we know, the son thinks a day of his hard labor is more worthy of celebration. Lame, isn't it? Yep, doers are party poopers!

17 The Initiative Is With Who?

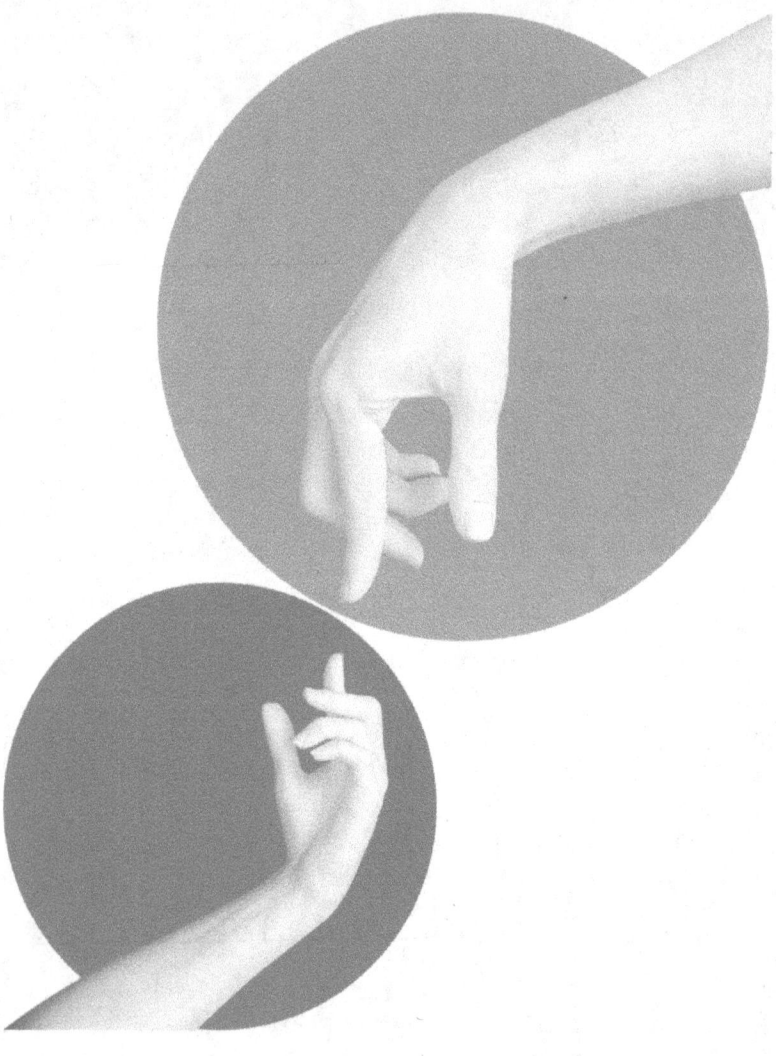

Figure 17: *Father, Stretch Out Your Hand*

And he said to him, "Son, you are always with me, and all that is mine is yours. It was fitting to celebrate and be glad, for your brother was dead, and is alive; he was lost, and is found."

— **Luke 15:31-32**

I tell you, there will be more joy in heaven over one sinner who repents than over ninety-nine righteous persons who need no repentance.

— **Luke 15:7**

The two groups in Jesus' audience are now utterly lost in the profound responses of the father to the two sons of the parable. The sinners are lost at the thought of the father having nothing but a warm embrace and celebration for the younger son. Meanwhile, the religious leaders are confused by the reality of how this father cares more about the elder son's relationship with him than his work for him. Furthermore, how odd it is for the father to delight in a bum who hasn't done the slightest thing to merit it. To be sure, the different groups are questioning within the depths of their being, "You mean, the father here is God? You got to be kidding me! You're telling us this is how God is like? He's our Father, and a compassionate one?"

It's our question too. If answered with a "Yes"—which it's clear that it is—how do we live life? If the meaning in life is not about what we do, then what is it? How do we become right, if not based on how we perform? Verse 32 is the answer to all of humanity's pounding question on how to become right when there's clearly something wrong with us:

> And he said to him, "Son, you are always with me, and all that is mine is yours. It was fitting to celebrate and be glad, for this your brother was dead, and is alive; he was lost, and is found."

What's the word the father uses to describe the son's relationship with him? It's with. We would think he would say, "You have always obeyed me," but that's neither the reality nor the issue here. My friends, it has never been the issue regarding how God loves you and how you are made right. The father says, "You are always with me," and now your brother is with me. To which the religious think, "Wait, you're telling me with is a bigger deal than do? Is being close to you a bigger deal than doing for you always?" The lawbreakers are thinking, "Really? Is that how God thinks about me?" Yep. It's with, not do.

Let me ask you, which brother did the father love more? The conclusion is, "He loved both of them equally, but only one finally found a fulfilling relationship with him." If we think that what we do is the lens through which God views us, we could follow the logic that the older you are, the more hopeless you are. Because God only knows how much you're "missing the mark" compounds each year of your life! But Jesus says that we are all hopeless. So, Jesus decided to remove sin altogether out of the equation. He pulled do out of the equation by fulfilling all of the law's requirements for us single-handedly (see Matthew 5:17-20).

Doing is entirely off the table. How do I know this? Apostle Paul lived a life at the beginning that did more outright harm than you or I might ever do—killing people (Christians) in the name of Jihad. Paul went from a religious terrorist, hating Jesus and His people, to emulating Jesus' ministry and life. And so Paul could write:

While we were still weak, at the right time, Christ died for the ungodly. For one will scarcely die for a righteous person—though perhaps for a good person one would dare even to die—but God shows his love for us in that while we were still sinners, Christ died for us (Romans 5:6-8).

Paul, having been ambushed by the love of Jesus on his way to kill more Christians (see Acts 9), concludes that God doesn't have the same kind of love people have for you or the love you have for yourself. The love God shows us is not our love; it's not people's love, nor is it culture's love for us: it is "His love." While you and I were still sinning our brains out—while we were still living for ourselves out of our desires and compulsions—God loved us. Before you had the opportunity to do or not do, God loved you. God took the do—took our failure to do or "missing of the mark"—away by His doing (His sacrificial love to bear our penalty of death) so that we may be made alive. (We will talk about this in length in chapter twenty.) All we need to do is turn around to face the Father, and He will meet you where you're at and bring you home.

It's essential to know how the enemy tricks us into viewing ourselves at any given moment in ways that have little to do with who we are. If you allow self-pity in, the god you make will be too small or too far away to help—you don't merit his help. Of equal danger is thinking that there's no need to be saved from your pigpen because you've got it under control—after all, you're the "answer." Even if one knows something is wrong with them but thinks they must earn help and acceptance, they treat our compassionate Father as a liar—and that's blasphemy. Undoubtedly, the Father's heart breaks when we don't embrace Him for who He is. If God is not your Father, then you're not His child and are far away from the Solution.

In short, if you don't have some idea of God being your compassionate Father, you'll never understand who you are and will never come home. You'll never have an idea of your beloved-ness if you don't have the right image of God. As Blaise Pascal writes, "God made man in his own image, and man returned the compliment."[1] Unknowingly, we project our attitudes and feelings towards ourselves on God. But we shouldn't "assume that He feels about us the way we feel about ourselves," adds Manning.[2]

By confusing the content of our character with God's, we've become one of two people: 1) A child who seeks acceptance by their actions outside the home, or 2) A child who seeks acceptance by their actions done in the name of home. Both, as reflected in the two sons, are wrong. Both say they need to induce God's love, that the initiative must be theirs, not God's. Manning puts it like this, "Their image of God necessarily locks them into a theology of works."[3]

Unknowingly, we may be serving our false concept of God and not the Father. We think of idolatry as people worshiping beasts, stones, statues, or trees. However, any idea we follow that's not God the Father as revealed in the Bible is idolatry.

Some of us believe that God leaves us when we make

mistakes, and that He is the sheriff enforcing His Law. Even if you know you are His child, you will find no rest in being one with this mindset. Because you must strive to be good enough, which you can't. No wonder so many "Christians" are still enslaved, miserable, and their presence is insufferable!

History testifies that religion and religious people tend to be narrow, perfectionistic, idealistic, and neurotic, oppressing others by what Alan Jones calls "a terrorist spirituality."[4] Instead of bringing life, joy, and wonderment, religion often chokes them out. Life is codified, and God is cribbed.[5] The Bible is then read like a book of laws and not the love story that it is. The message of God's prophets and the agreements founded on God's grace with the Israelite patriarchs are forgotten.

It's why in his book *Why I Am Not A Christian*, philosopher Bertrand Russell wrote, "The intolerance that spread over the world with the advent of Christianity is one of its most curious features."[6]

How true! The broken cogs of religion surface in every encounter Jesus had with the Pharisees. Where the Pharisees insisted on the weightiness of God's Law by dismissing people's dignity and needs as ill-relevant, Jesus emphasized that law was not an end in itself but the means to an end. Living by God's dos and don'ts was meant to be an expression of our love for God and neighbor; any form of doing that stood in the way of such love stood in the way of God.[7] Jesus said in Matthew 5:17, "Do not think that I have come to abolish the Law or the Prophets; I have not come to abolish them but to fulfill them." What Jesus was offering was not a new law but a new attitude toward it. This challenged the Jewish religious system to which the Pharisees subscribed.

Not surprisingly, the elder son of Jesus' parable represents the Pharisees' attitude towards obedience to the law. Their attitude is that keeping the law somehow allows God to like them. Or, as Manning puts it, "Divine acceptance is secondary and is conditioned by the Pharisee's behavior."[8] They make first things secondary and put secondary things first. The elder son shows all of us that what intrudes on God's relationship with human beings is our hollow morality and false uprightness. And what intrudes on the Pharisee is the gospel of grace, the reality of being accepted and loved by God before living the law of love. "We love because he first loved us" (1 John 4:19). But the thinking of the Pharisee can't accept this. The initiative is theirs, they believe! God is distant, and He's eager to find fault. That kind of image of an insufferable God fundamentally locks them into a life of doing. And since there's always imperfection, "the Pharisee must pursue a lifestyle that minimizes mistakes" and make blaming, accusing, and guilt-tripping others their mission.[9] Blame is a defensive substitute for an honest examination of life; it's a way of turning our minds away from our errors by endlessly reciting tortured variations of the law.

Once put this way, the elder brother's blaming outrage in the parable is expected. It wasn't just the young brother who was at fault for being wasteful but also the father who invited his brother home for a celebration before any initiative of the younger brother. The father is viewed especially wrong when the elder son had taken the initiative and never felt that he was celebrated.

Again, if we think God seems to give parties benevolently but impulsively withdraws them too, we become like the resentful older son—"Dad is just crazy and unfair." When we experience good times, we think God is pleased, and we stand accepted. To us, wealth, inner peace, health, and provision represent acceptance. But when we are pinned down by life, we may perceive it to be evidence of God's displeasure and rejection of us. Soon God becomes just as inconsistent, unpredictable, demanding, inconsiderate, and deceptive as we are. Under such a god, to be sure, our noses are rubbed in our sins, and retaliation will be seen everywhere.

Identifying with the younger son more than the older in Jesus' parable might be a natural response, given how we may share in similar hardships and shame which marked the young son's journey. However, we, too, share in the older son's defective default. We try to make ourselves right by our performance, finding merit in it, and justifying our entire being on it. Like the older brother, our work has taken us away from meaningful events and relationships happening at home. Instead, we set expectations for what people ought to do, and we have the same ones for ourselves. But, as we've seen with the elder son, doers miss out on the good things happening in the now. Being so focused on how things "ought" to be done, we miss what good things God is doing right in front of us—His bestowal of blessings, joy, and forgiveness. Because we can't see these, much less receive them, we become detached, miserable, and resentful.

To paraphrase Manning, how is it that we've come to imagine that Christianity is made up of mostly what we do for God?[10] Do we consider this to be good news, to have received a kingdom with a King who reigns with a list of dos and don'ts? Allow the words of Manning to impact your soul:

> *Is the kingdom that He proclaimed to be nothing more than a community of men and women who go to church on Sunday, take an annual spiritual retreat, read their*

Bibles every now and then, vigorously oppose abortion, don't watch x-rated movies, never use vulgar language, smile a lot, hold doors open for people, root for the favorite team, and get along with everybody? Is that why Jesus went through the bleak and bloody horror of Calvary? Is that why He emerged in shattering glory from the tomb? Is that why He poured out His Holy Spirit on the church? To make nicer men and women with better morals? The gospel is absurd and the life of Jesus is meaningless unless we believe that He lived, died, and rose again with but one purpose in mind: to make brand-new creations. Not to make people with better morals, but to create a community of prophets and professional lovers, men and women who would surrender to the mystery of the fire of the Spirit that burns within, who would live in ever greater fidelity to the omnipresent Word of God, who would enter into the center of it all, the very heart and mystery of Christ, into the center of the flame that consumes, purifies, and sets everything aglow with peace, joy, boldness, and extravagant, furious love. This, my friends, is what it really means to be a Christian.[11]

Our relationship with God never begins with what we do for God, nor will it be sustained by what we do. It always starts with what God has done for us and never ends with what we have done, as long as we come home to Him in repentance.

In the book of Ephesians (2:10), as New Testament believers we are informed: "For we are his workmanship, created in Christ Jesus for good works, which God prepared beforehand, that we should walk in them." Note how we don't become the workmanship or the masterpiece because we produced good works—that's being self-made. No. We become the workmanship of God to share in God's good works. A slave works under the threat of pain and loss. A son works under the discipline of loving instruction that he may share in his father's work. It's for this reason the Holy Spirit was poured out. The spirit of sonship is the ability given by the Holy Spirit to approach God as Father. A slave operates in that which scares but a son serves in what brings security. As slaves, we work with no honor. As sons, we are honored and invited to join in the work. There is ownership, freedom, and peace for those who stay in the presence of the Father.

If we internalized this truth and made this the core reality of our being, we would stand utterly transformed and indistinguishable from His light, set aglow, and forever freed. If you get this from your head to your heart, it will impact every part of your life—fulfillment rests in ending our love affair with slavery and living out of pure being.

Journal Entry: One Busy, The Other In Love

"Being with, not doing do" is a truth that we may accept about our spiritual salvation. Still, we may not necessarily think it relevant to pull this truth down into the ordinariness of everyday life. Yet, it's what Jesus made evident to two sisters at a dinner they hosted. Luke's book records the event:

> *Now, as they went on their way, Jesus entered a village. And a woman named Martha welcomed him into her house. And she had a sister called Mary, who sat at the Lord's feet and listened to his teaching. But Martha was distracted with much serving. And she went up to him and said, "Lord, do you not care that my sister has left me to serve alone? Tell her then to help me." But the Lord answered her, "Martha, Martha, you are anxious and troubled about many things, but one thing is necessary. Mary has chosen the good portion, which will not be taken away from her"* (Luke 10:38-42).

Martha has responded to a social obligation. Being a homeowner, she has invited Jesus and His disciples into her home to show hospitality. Her sister Mary reacted differently. Mary is at the feet of Jesus, enamored with Jesus and His teachings as a Rabbi. She's listening to a man who broke social order—welcoming a woman into participation in discussion with men. Probably in a frenzy, social obligations got the best of Martha's humanity as she was dead-set on proving Mary to be of no help—a bum.[12] Martha could have politely invited her sister into the kitchen, but like a law-keeper, Martha bypasses her sister and rushes to "expose" her to Jesus. Martha is trying to get Jesus to stand up for her expectations.

Oddly enough, Jesus responds to cool her down but doesn't bless her with extra hands to work the tables. "Martha, Martha," He weighs in, "you are anxious and troubled about many things, but one thing is necessary." Her perceived need was out of focus and misplaced, leaving her stressed out and a nervous wreck. It is not hard to believe that Martha's state of being in this event may have very well been the state of her inner being all the time. As Trent C. Butler writes, "Her life was out of focus, dedicated to fulfilling the world's expectations rather than Jesus'."[13]

While she concerned herself with the perceived need to perform socially, Martha was neglecting life's one essential need: to hear the voice of God and be utterly enthralled to be with Him. Jesus reveals how Maratha is taking a temporary position in life that will be taken away from her. In contrast, her sister Mary had "chosen the good portion, which will not be taken away from her."

The main idea here is how commitment to Jesus is more important than all other obligations. We must not choose to follow the world's expectations, and all who have must change our priorities to listen to the voice of God. All else is secondary. Each day presents us with such a decision—to be with Jesus or be busy and distract ourselves to the point of missing life's vision completely.

18 To Be Or Not To Be

Figure 18: *Time Passes By*

And he said to him, "Son, you are always with me, and all that is mine is yours. It was fitting to celebrate and be glad, for your brother was dead, and is alive; he was lost, and is found."

— **Luke 15:31-32**

As it is said, "Today, if you hear his voice, do not harden your hearts as in the rebellion."

— **Hebrews 3:15**

With the words of verse 32, Jesus ends the parable of *The Prodigal Son*. There's no resolution to the father's and his firstborn's tension. We might conclude that we have misplaced the end somewhere. We're hanging on the edge of our seats, looking for the elder son's response. But the abruptness of the ending is purposeful—sharpening the point which Jesus has made. The story is about the Heavenly Father and us. We get to finish the elder son's response because we are him.

Kenneth E. Bailey, a commentator fluent in Arabic and a specialist in Middle-Eastern literature, gives us the parable's linguistic structure, which reveals why Jesus left it unfinished. The form is a systematic kind of mirrored pattern [ABCD-DCBA] called a *chiasm*—poetic parallelism, a typical storytelling device in Middle-Eastern prose. (See next page.)

Part 1: The Younger Brother[1]
- A. Death
  - B. All Is Lost
    - C. Rejection
      - D. The Problem
      - D. The Solution
    - C. Acceptance
  - B. All Is Restored
- A. Resurrection

Part 2: The Older Brother
- A. He Stands Aloof
  - B. Your Brother; Peace (a feast); Anger
    - C. Costly Love
      - D. My Actions, My Pay
      - D. His Actions, His Pay
    - C. Costly Love
  - B. Your Brother; Safe (a feast); Joy!
- A. (The Missing Ending)

We're supposed to notice that there's an end missing. And it is left to us to decide how it should end. In the law-keepers apparent distaste for Jesus that led to the eventual murder of Jesus, we could say they complete the story with "We Stand Aloof."

And this is what I find amazing. It wasn't the thugs, rapists, and thieves who killed Jesus. He was nailed to a timber of torture by the well-scrubbed hands of the deeply religious. The most respected members of society were the ones who murdered God's Son in the name of religiosity. It was those people who knew that knowledge could be power in the religious realm.[2] Like the elder son of the parable, they were fearful when others were free, cynical when given negative feedback, and paranoid when challenged.

Could it be that it's the world's game of one-upmanship in a system of dos and don'ts that permits the exchange of a lie for a truth? Could it be that the same system introduces a spirit of competition, rivalry, and oppression incompatible with the unselfconsciousness of the child of God? I am beginning to understand that those estranged from the Father are caught up in the power games of life. They are like the elder son, who ostensibly live hallowed lives and have every semblance of success on the outside. But they are, in effect, pharisees who seek to master God rather than be conquered by the Love of God. They want to be god, not be with God.

I believe the life of the elder son, the Pharisee, and all who follow their example, live in "the agnosticism of inattention."[3] This agnosticism isn't made up by a consistent denial of a personal God but by a kind of disbelief arising from inattention to God's presence. It's saying that we know God because we know all of His commandments yet deny His sacred presence in daily life. It happens when I sink into unawareness, excluding Christ from things I'd rather enjoy alone. It's also taking praise for my merit when I know I am nothing without the Father. It is denying myself the courage to have faith, preferring to rationalize with my intellect when something challenges my understanding of how God works. It's living under the bombardment of daily tasks that demand my attention or having a brief moment of shallow prayer or a sterile conversation. It's in treating life as a series of disconnected events, with nothing to see beyond appearances. It's my use of time, money, and talents as if God is distant as if He doesn't want to be involved in the things in which I am involved. So we respond to the beautiful arrangement of events, a word of good news, a tender touch, and emotions, with passivity. It's when I see a young couple declaring to love forever, or a person saying "I heard from God," and I say cynically, "I'm wiser, more mature than that. I see things now as they truly are."

This approach to life is insufferable: it's the life of a slave, the life of a Pharisee, claiming to know God but never experiencing true intimacy with Him.

For life to change from enslavement to being the beloved Child of God, there must be an awareness and a sense of wonderment for His involvement with us. This is hard in the churning of daily life.

The Nazareth Syndrome

To His hometown of Nazareth Jesus began to bring to life the famous promises from Isaiah by literally fleshing out the announcement that the Messiah had come. How did they receive His announcement? Did they jump with joy? "Praise God! Our help is here! The promised Messiah which all past generations longed for is in front of us, and we know Him!" Nope. They sat there in an attitude of contempt, thinking of the prophetic insights that came out of His mouth and snidely saying, "Is this not Joseph's son? Don't we know His mother, his brothers? He's just one of us" (see Luke 4:22; Mark 6:2-3)—making supernatural things commonplace. This attitude is what some have called "the Nazareth syndrome."

The Nazareth syndrome is resistant to change because we don't accept the Jesus who meets us in our daily, ordinary life. It's when we get accustomed to having Jesus as a part of us. We somehow lose sight of His divinity, and we assume we can put things off and take Him for granted. Then we settle down where we are and resist any new change.

Jesus points out that in Elijah's day, many starving widows were in Israel. Still, only one was fed supernaturally—and she was not even an Israelite but a foreigner of Sidon (see Luke 4:26). As she gathered sticks for a fire to cook a meal and eat with her son, intending to die, Elijah approached her, saying:

> *Do not fear; go and do as you have said. But first, make me a little cake of it and bring it to me, and afterward make something for yourself and your son. For thus says the Lord, the God of Israel, "The jar of flour shall not be spent, and the jug of oil shall not be empty, until the day that the Lord sends rain upon the earth"* (1 Kings 17:13-14).

The widow was to do what she always did, make bread—nothing more mundane than to live an ordinary day. And when she did, she relied on the miracle of multiplied olive oil and grain meal. She hungered with her son no more. Jesus was saying, "There were many starving widows in the land, but only one was open to God."

Again, He said, many lepers were in Israel at the time of Elisha, but only one was cleansed and made whole (see Luke 4:27). He was an army captain from Syria, an enemy of Israel. Although Naaman was a proud man, he finally listened to his servant and obeyed the prophet's directions. He became willing to humble himself and bathe in the ordinary, muddy waters of the Jordan river to be cleansed (see 2 Kings 5:13, 14). Others too could have been healed, but to bathe in regular waters appeared insignificant to them. Thus they missed out on God's extraordinary gift.

The elder son of Jesus' parable could have been healed from his troubles and eaten his fill at his father's feast like his prodigal brother, but the occasion seemed insignificant to him.

We can ask ourselves why are there so many marriages that break up after years of walking together in the Lord? Why do we have so many people just enduring their marriages, putting up with one another? Those situations are because people have stopped the process of change in themselves and their relationships. They no longer have hope, or no longer want change. The relationships are dead-end streets, dark places in their hearts. They have no real awareness that things could be better. There is no sense of wonderment of what God is doing in each situation or trial. The enemy comes at these weak points and says, "Why accept anything else?" or "You'll never make it." When we no longer cry for the Spirit, we begin only to see from the eyes of self.

King David writes, "I would have fainted unless I had believed to see the goodness of the LORD in the land of the living" (Psalm 27:13). David says that he wouldn't have survived if not for his certainty that he would see the goodness (in the wildest sense, beauty) of God within the present world. To help him in his time of need, David held on to faith, looking for what God was doing in the present, which he knew was before him.

There's something near to the heart of God about the common, the everyday and ordinary. The ever-present heart of God is evident in the name of Christ—"Emmanuel" or "God with us." It's what Manning describes as the ongoing miracle of the gospel. It's Christ who is in our every moment, tracking us, abiding in us, and offering Himself to us as a companion for the journey.[4] As Manning shares, "At every moment of our existence, God offers us this good news."[5]

For us to experience the good news, we aren't required to find good news or do the work of finding where God might be. That's what a Pharisee would do. And that is what the elder son did. Once he heard the good news shared to him by his father, he responded with his opinion of what good news would be as if he really knew better. In actuality, it's only by being found by God, listening to and trusting in the good news He shares. Not until then, will we have experiential knowledge of the good news that transforms our daily lives.

Jesus' statement of how the prodigal "was lost, and is found" represents this thought. When you become found, it's not that you found yourself, but someone else did. So, the quest in our daily lives is not to find ourselves or find what God is doing, but rather to let ourselves be found by God (cf. 2 Chronicles 16:9).

Where The Voice Of God Is

The Nazareth syndrome tends to block the good news from being experienced by those working out their scheduled agendas. Instead, the good news is experienced by those allowing themselves to be found by God in the words He speaks. The good news is not reserved for those who give themselves over to the hard discipline of doing, but for those listening out of their hunger and thirst. Prophet Elijah experiences this truth in 1 Kings 18 and 19.

Elijah is best known for being God's representative on Mount Carmel when he and the people of Israel defeated "the four hundred and fifty prophets of Baal and the four hundred prophets of Asherah," who ate at the table of their enemy. Elijah challenged the godless to a BBQ cook-off—in the sense that a cow would become cooked. The challenge for each group was to call on the name of their god, asking for fire to come down from heaven and consume the offering. It's pretty odd until you realize how roasting a cow was ordinary for the two groups as they both believed in animal sacrifices to please their deity.

The record shows that the godless prophets did everything to gain attention and fire from their god, short of killing themselves. They shouted, danced, screamed louder, and even began to cut themselves with swords and spears until they were standing in their blood. To add to their anxiety, Elijah began to taunt them. "Shout louder! Surely he is a god! Perhaps he is deep in thought, relieving himself, busy, or traveling. Maybe he is sleeping and must be awakened" (verse 27). In this bit of smack talk, Elijah reveals their state of mind: *Our god is far away, and we need to find him, so we need to do something dramatic and loud, or else he won't find us.* Their high stake challenge of their false god's ability ended in raw meat.

Elijah offers an alternative. At the evening sacrifice, the prophet Elijah stepped forward and prayed two simple sentences (verses 36 and 37). The Hebrew text expresses that he drew near to God and more or less pleaded, "Reveal yourself so they may be acquainted with You, and know that I did this because of my relationship with You." For the false prophets, this is a very different approach to God. It's relational. It's not based on performance or radical commitment to impress. It's not an event occurring out of the need for something to be done for a relationship with God. But something is done to demonstrate an already established relationship. And God delivered a roaring cookout that day. We're told:

> *Then the fire of the Lord fell and consumed the burnt offering and the wood and the stones and the dust, and licked up the water that was in the trench. And when all the people saw it, they fell on their faces and said, "The Lord, he is God; the Lord, he is God"* (verses 38-39).

It's as though Elijah is a son who brings his father to a classroom on Parent's Day to reveal His identity through His work. It's like a second-grade boy bringing his dad, who's a fireman, to school to start a fire and put it out, demonstrating his work for all to see.

But even in this spectacular event of God revealing Himself to the passive audience of humanity, something goes unchanged in Elijah.

After Elijah's most significant day as a prophet, his life becomes endangered as a bounty marks his head. Running away from assassins for a full day, he finds himself resting in the shade of a tree where he prays a cowardly prayer: "I have had enough, Lord. Take my life. I am no better than my ancestors" (1 Kings 19:5). God sends an angel and feeds him some hot bread and a jar of water. That night he hides in a cave. Afterward, God more or less says, "Elijah, what on My green earth are you doing here?" Elijah's response was a self-pitying recitation of how much he had done for God. Then, unexpectedly, God doesn't address him but says, "Go out and stand on the mountain in the presence of the Lord, for the Lord is about to pass by." What happens next is confusing:

> And behold, the Lord passed by, and a great strong wind tore the mountains and broke in pieces the rocks before the Lord, but the Lord was not in the wind. And after the wind an earthquake, but the Lord was not in the earthquake. And after the earthquake, a fire, but the Lord was not in the fire. And after the fire, the sound of a low whisper. And when Elijah heard it, he wrapped his face in his cloak and went out and stood at the entrance of the cave. And behold, there came a voice to him and said, "What are you doing here, Elijah?" He said, "I have been very jealous for the Lord, the God of hosts. For the people of Israel have forsaken your covenant, thrown down your altars, and killed your prophets with the sword, and I, even I only, am left, and they seek my life, to take it away." And the Lord said to him, "Go, return on your way to the wilderness of

> *Damascus. And when you arrive, you shall anoint Hazael to be king over Syria... Yet I will leave seven thousand in Israel, all the knees that have not bowed to Baal, and every mouth that has not kissed him"* (1 Kings 19:11-18).

It's obvious now that God did not send an angel to Elijah to make him feel better about running away but to keep the prophet alive until he was able enough to hear the Lord. Then God came to call him lovingly. His method of speaking was most unusual and, in a way, least expected. Not in large, boisterous ways. Not in sudden, shattering changes. But as a low whisper, hardly audible. His voice spoke tenderly.

God is making a point. "I speak differently than the world." God doesn't advertise, make marketable, or blast attention-grabbing sound bites. Neither is His voice demanding like the ones of the world. Instead, it is tender and speaks to those who listen. God is also telling us through Elijah's experience, "To be with me, you must be different."

Nouwen's realization of God's approach to being with us reveals this profound truth:

> *Now I wonder whether I have sufficiently realized that God has been trying to find me, know me, and love me during all this time. The question is not "How am I to find God?" but "How am I to let myself be found by him?" The question is not "How am I to know God?" but "How am I to let myself be known by God?" And, finally, the question is not "How am I to love God?" but*

"How am I to let myself be loved by God?"[6]

Maybe all this time, we've tried, as the elder son of the parable did, to find our Father in things that have no business with Him. The clamor of life isn't of God's nature. Neither is His Truths found in excessive mass, intensity, energy, or density. No, it's more usual for the voice of God to be in the invisible. We can only hear God's voice and follow Him into what pleases Him in the contemplative life. While busyness and inattentiveness distract us from God's presence, contemplation places us in God's presence. God is most glorified when we are most satisfied in Him and not necessarily when we're doing impressive things in His name. When we are away from God in our efforts, even if our efforts are expended on good things, we become the emotionally estranged elder son in the mind and heart.

If the good we do stands in the way of listening to the voice of God, how good is it?

Consider the words of Jesus recorded in Matthew's gospel:

Not everyone who says to me, "Lord, Lord," will enter the kingdom of heaven, but the one who does the will of my Father who is in heaven. On that day, many will say to me, "Lord, Lord, did we not prophesy in your name, and cast out demons in your name, and do many mighty works in your name?" And then will I declare to them, "I never knew you; depart from me, you workers of lawlessness" (Matthew 7:21-23).

To be found by God in our ordinary life, having faith that He speaks words to you with all compassion love can hold, is a spiritual truth.[7] We experience the presence of God in our simple presence in life, not exactly in spiritual highs or our spectacular deeds. Once there, your only desire should be to make the truth "You are my beloved" send ripples throughout every corner of your being.[8] Until then, we're like the elder son who no longer hears what Boris Pasternak called "the inward music" of their beloved-ness.

Journal Entry: Doers Often Miss The Vision

Now he was teaching in one of the synagogues on the Sabbath. And behold, there was a woman who had had a disabling spirit for eighteen years. She was bent over and could not fully straighten herself. When Jesus saw her, he called her over and said to her, "Woman, you are freed from your disability." And he laid his hands on her, and immediately she was made straight, and she glorified God. But the ruler of the synagogue, indignant since Jesus had healed on the Sabbath, said to the people, "There are six days in which work ought to be done. Come on those days and be healed, and not on the Sabbath day." Then the Lord answered him, "You hypocrites! Does not each of you on the Sabbath untie his ox or his donkey from the manger and lead it away to water it? And ought not this woman, a daughter of Abraham whom Satan bound for eighteen years, become loosened from this bond on the Sabbath day?" As he said these things, all his adversaries were put to shame, and all the people rejoiced at all the glorious things that were done by him.

— Luke 13:10-17

Observations:

I find Jesus teaching within a synagogue—a meeting place or prayer hall—on the Sabbath. Here's what I know about the Sabbath:

- The Sabbath (Saturday) is mentioned eighty-nine times in the Old Testament alone.

- It was a day chosen by God Himself on which He took a rest after reviewing His six days of creation. The Lord wanted humans made in His image to set aside that same day of the week to rest in the pattern of the divine example.

- Keeping the Sabbath separate from all other days is meant to be pleasant and refreshing—resting in God—but never a burden.

The Sabbath is intended for us to review our work and contemplate the purpose for which we were bought into the world. Essentially, the Sabbath was used as a day of observance set apart to the Lord in reflection. In addition, it would act as a time for the renewal or recommitment to the state or way of life already chosen.

Considering the past work week, we review our choices in light of our commitment to walk with God in faithfulness during that week. The day was more or less reserved to take stock of how one's living out of a particular lifestyle revealed... whether or not one was responding to God's faith call.[9] The Sabbath, therefore, was a profitable day in regards to the inner life, which enabled people to live a holy—a whole/centered/pure—life in their situations and environment. The understanding was that one's progress in living out their lives in God would be in direct proportion to the surrender of their self-love and their own will and interests.[10]

The "ruler" in the text of Luke 13 is a man chosen to care for the physical arrangements of the synagogue services. Being a religious leader presiding over this local synagogue, he knows his religion and is ready to use it. Like most all law-keepers, I can imagine how he loved to practice law in the meeting house for all to see—the more people shamed, the better. So he confronts Jesus for calling out a disabled woman from His audience and restoring her to health through casting out a demonic spirit—this woman was in prison within her own body.

I'm looking at the Greek word used for "saw" here: "when Jesus saw her." I think it can be translated more accurately as "became aware" or "did not forget." So, it may mean that for Jesus to see her meant that He didn't forget about her in her need.

The ruler is upset that Jesus is aware of the woman—having a relationship with her (practically speaking). He confronts Jesus indirectly by frantically addressing Jesus' audience—"There are six days in which work ought to be done. Come on those days and be healed, and not on the Sabbath day."[11] The guy is indirectly telling off Jesus' audience for witnessing His dedication to the human need. Why? It was the wrong day to care for people because maybe Sabbath for him was "Program Day."

Jesus now confronts him directly: "You religious people are all the same—hypocrites! Don't you care for your beloved animals, leading them to water on a Sabbath? How about this poor woman who needs care—she's a victim who needs freedom and rest. She is the beloved daughter of God. Should God have less compassion for her than your precious animals?!"

Conclusion:

In their misinterpretation of God's vision for keeping the Sabbath, the religious leaders of Jesus' day focused on the program, not the people—as all professional doers tend to do. I'm finding here in Luke's record the dangers of being dedicated to the pursuit of doing rather than pursuing a relationship with God and others. The man became infuriated at what he perceived as unworthy behavior—dedication to people over the program. "How dare you break our law! You know we can't work on the Sabbath. The teachers have long established that healing is work." His objection sounds familiar, doesn't it—It's DO not WITH!

Jesus reveals to these religious people that they have misunderstood what God's work is, and the whole point of the Sabbath. His dedication to God meant meeting human needs, while commitment to religion—a system of do—treated people like enslaved animals. Jesus' healing presence towards the disabled and His rebuke of the leaders was a battle cry against the system of do. We can imagine this was a drop mic moment for Jesus, and the hush that fell over the humbled religious leaders broke with praise and joy as the crowd roared. It was time to celebrate what Jesus was doing—being a defender of the individual against the religious and political system.

We learn from this occasion that doers miss the vision: It's about being with people in all their needs—relationships—not about protecting and completing programs—performance.

Journal Entry: Recovering Passion

I'm learning that the greatness of God's majesty is not magnified in hollow efforts to keep commandments—every religion does that. Hollow works may make you look moral, but it doesn't make God look great. Rather, the greatness of God's majesty is exalted when you're satisfied in Him more than anything, especially when you're suffering. Until I realize that the ultimate essence of evil is the failure to be satisfied in God, I won't be able to devote my life to magnifying God. Just wondering… how often do I try to be good without any attention to being satisfied in God?

More than likely, I'm fighting the battle at the level of deeds: "More of that," and "Less of this." Satan is laughing that I'm fighting on a front that I can never succeed in. The battle is in my heart. It's really deep there. What do I love? What do I cherish? What am I satisfied by? Am I fighting that kind of battle? That's the battle that may give rise to all that is good and kills all that is evil.

So, what I need is passion. I need to recover my passion for God. Because passion is about the majesty of God, and I'll never make much of the majesty of God until I learn that the ultimate essence of evil is preferring anything to God (see Psalm 90:14).

His love instills a new passion within, which carries out the desires of His Spirit. These passions never enslave me but free me to experience the present risen-ness of Christ, the author, and perfecter of our life. Jesus shares with me a promise between Himself, the Father, and His Children. It's a promise of His blood that covers my inability and failure to maintain a relationship with God. This is not a need of God for us to have a relationship with Him, and it is not a demand. His forever call for us to love Him for who He is to us is a passionate cry that has never been heard from any other god. I have not known a god to ever inquire of me how I feel about Him. But the Father who created all life, however, asks if I care about Him, if there's a passion for Him. And if passion at its root means "to act in suffering for," what suffering do I endure in life for the Father? If Jesus voluntarily lays Himself open to me, allowing Himself to be intimately affected by me, He's in a state of passion for me. Jesus is heartbroken and weeps over my not receiving Him as the one He wants to be to me.

Do I feel the same about Him? Am I like Jesus' disciple John who named himself "the one whom Jesus loved"? Do I allow myself to be so deeply affected by Jesus that I act out the different reality my relationship with Him creates in passion? Do I incline my head on the heart of Jesus, like John who was leaning on Jesus' bosom while eating with Him for the last time? (see John 13:23) Do I listen to the rhythm of God's heart and make it the music I dance to? Is this too radical? Too intimate? No, it's the mystery of the incarnated love of God. The term "my little children" is a term of affection to delight in. There's no longer any other way to live as a child of God than to delight in His affection for us. So, no longer will I live on borrowed emotions, stumbling through life, never tasting life deeply as one uniquely valued and loved. I no longer want words of truth just to engage my mind and not engage my heart that is elsewhere and divided. Instead, I want my engaged mind to be awakened to the reality of God's love for me, so that awareness of this truth will flow into my heart, that my heart will engage, be affected by love, and awaken passion.

No longer do I want an ecstatic trance, high emotion, or sanguine stance towards life. On the contrary, I want a desperate longing for God—true transformation. I want a resolution to no longer to linger in pious rules and temporal highs within this world. I wish to live out the truth of my beloved-ness. Only the love of Christ will compel me then! And transformation will surely come about in living a unified personality, in a state of passionate awareness.

19 The Ordinary Christian Life

Figure 19: *Child-Like*

I'm afraid too many Christians look like shriveled old prunes. They endlessly trudge along with frowns and furrowed brows, bearing death in their bodies and trying to justify their existence. They're anchored, like the elder son, to their needs, heralding their arrival and standing on a gaudy soapbox to demand attention from others. They find their center of gravity in who they know, in the conferring of honors, or the illusion of worthiness based on performance, all of which attempts to eclipse the love of God, the source of all life. Their existence on earth doesn't signify to them that God loves them. They don't understand, as do all the prodigals who return, that they may give glory to God by their simple presence in life, in being themselves. They may know that God is their Father in the sense that He is their creator, but they do not know Him as a Father who longs to be with them, yearning to hear their voice. Because of this, their lives are miserable, insufferable, a project and not a passion, a field to work in and not a party to dance in. Their potential is untouched. Life is strangled, and growth is stifled. Joy becomes slaughtered. Their smoldering wick is snuffed out, their bruised reed crushed. Intimacy is estranged from them.

As I grow in faith, I realize that anchoring myself to the reality that "I am beloved" brings me life and freedom, transforming my whole being. The fact that God has created us for union with Himself is not some inspiring idea or comforting lie: it is the original purpose of our lives. Being the beloved of God is our identity. And living in the awareness of our beloved-ness is central to the Christian life—the axis on which our lives revolve.

"Who am I?", the question that once tormented us because we answered with do, becomes the question leading us to wholeness and freedom when answered with "I am the one loved by God." Our longing to know who we really are—which is the source of all our discontentment—will never be satisfied until our identity rests in God's relentless compassion for us revealed in Christ Jesus. Once in that knowledge, our "controlled frenzy" turns into a well-ordered existence, and death is transformed into resurrection. No longer do we move from crisis to crisis, but from victory to victory.

The indispensable condition for growing and maintaining the normal Christian life is having an awareness of our beloved-ness in the presence of God.

Awareness: The Normal State Of The Christian

Awareness, or being in the state of knowledge, is the first step in the normal Christian life. Without it, you'll live as the master of the pigpen or the slave in the field. As Apostle Paul says, "We know that our old self was crucified with him in order that the body of sin might be brought to nothing, so that we would no longer be enslaved to sin" (Romans 6:6). Knowing is the attainment of thought. It's not an intellectual pursuit. Knowing is the opening of your eyes to see what Christ sees. I have never known any Christian that has done it by merely obtaining intellectual knowledge upon entering the ordinary Christian life. Each will relate their first-hand experience with Christ. I don't mean that the sinner becomes a Christian by experience because that would go against God's Word. What I do mean is that each Christian who has ever gone deeper into their sanctification (set-apartness) has encountered Jesus in a uniquely intimate way paired with His Word. It's the rediscovery of the person and work of Jesus, with whom we come to feel, and not only understand, the way He loves and lives.

It's why Apostle Paul prayed for the Christians in Ephesus:

> *that the God of our Lord Jesus Christ, the Father of glory, may give you the Spirit of wisdom and of revelation in the knowledge of him, having the eyes of your hearts enlightened, that you may know what is the hope to which he has called you, what are the riches of his glorious inheritance in the saints, and what is the immeasurable greatness of his power toward us who believe, according to the working of his great might (Ephesians 1:17-19).*

Loosen Up

The Sons of Korah wrote the song "God Is Our Fortress" recorded in Psalm 46. In verse ten of the psalm, the voice of the Lord is calling out to us, "Be still, and know that I am God." The Hebrew word translated as the verb "be still" is a dynamic verb (רָפָה [rāp̄ah]). The action word is a command to slacken something. It carries with it the idea of relaxing, withdrawing, refraining, letting go, dropping, and doing nothing. But it's not the only action word. It's followed, actually introduced, by another Hebrew verb, a commanding action, "to know" (יָדַע [yāḏaʾ]). We may read the verse in Hebrew as, "to gain knowledge of God through every sense, you must relax your grip."

God tells us to "loosen up!"

Some of us have such a firm grip on life for fear of losing it that we choke the life out of it. With clenched fists, we stand in the world whenever we try to be in control. Nouwen describes this image of tightly clenched fists as "the desire to cling tightly to yourself, a greediness which betrays fear."[1] There's a story of a woman within a mental ward who went wild and clung to anything in her path. Doctors tore from her hands what they could, except for a tiny coin she clasped in her hand. As she was not willing to release the coin, two nurses had to pry open her strong but withering hand as a doctor recovered the coin. "It was as though she would lose her very self along with the coin. If they deprived her of that last possession, she would have nothing more and be nothing more. That was her fear."[2]

We, too, have clenched fists whenever our pride instructs us to prove a point to someone instead of leaving it up to God. Getting the last word in during an argument is a clenched fist. Demanding your way to be embraced as "the way" is a clenched fist. Resentment and hatred will form your hands into tight wads quicker than anything. Clenched fists of the spiritual and emotional kind are often reflected in occasions when our physical hands draw closed. Clenched fists are on display when you pound on the steering wheel after being insulted. It appears in a conversation with that person you're wary of when you have your arms crossed and hands folded tightly. No wonder the clenched fist is a symbol of power, defiance, and liberation worldwide!

Clenched fists are, at best, an act of self-preservation. It's experiencing hurt and rejection and closing ourselves to further exposure that may result in more wounds. It's also in scorning yourself and denying any affection because "you're unlovable." Finally, it's in being afraid of being touched, seen, or known. Adam and Eve had to have clenched fists in their grabbing of the fig leaves to keep themselves covered. Like we do in a card game, we hide our hands not to reveal our position.

While clenched fists reveal fear of losing what we hold, spreading our hands wide shows we accept the truth of who we are, dropping the false realities we have about ourselves. To receive the life and strength, God gives us the means to let go of the "life" and "strength" we may feel while viewing pornography. Let go of the lies we may use to manipulate and control people, processes, and outcomes when we feel out of control, powerless. Oddly, surrendering our ways in pursuit of "life," "strength," and "belonging" feels like losing everything and becoming nothing.

After a series of personal traumatic experiences, I remember how my body would close itself to the world. I couldn't leave home without shaking and my body becoming stiff. I noticed how I would have clenched fists under the pillow as I tried lying down for the night. After dreams of rejection and ridicule, I woke up to tightly bound fists. At times, I gazed into space, reliving trauma or pondering in resentment how someone treated me. It was in those times, my hands grew closed, often with white knuckles. I clung to the past as if I could change it or learn how to prevent something in the future. Soon, I saw all relationships as threats. Because they forced me to allow someone other than myself to walk into the center of my being and possibly touch things I would rather keep untouched.[3] Having intimacy was dangerous, so I was on the defense.

The bitterness, the hate, the jealousy, the hurt, the disappointment, and the desire for revenge are not just feelings but "treasures" we clutch in our hands, not knowing what to do if found without them. You hold onto them for dear life because to give them up would mean losing your very self. It would seem that to lose your hatred, victimhood, retaliation, or your cherished habit of self-gratification is to lose yourself. So we stand in a world with balled-up fists, closed to the One who wishes to help us and place blessing in our hands.[4]

Our question, therefore, becomes, "How do I open my hands?" Not by force. Neither will it be done by God. It's not repeated and artificial citations of prayer. Nor is it merely a decision. No, it's a long spiritual journey of trust founded in prayer that dispels the layers behind each clenched fist that took years of tension to build up.[5] As prayer seems painful and frightening, to be led to pray, it would help to listen carefully to the words of God spoken 70 times throughout time to every person needing to approach Him: "Do not be afraid… I am your reward. I have heard you, I am with you; I will bless you, keep you from sinning; I will protect you. Give me anything too hard for you, and I will fight for you. I won't leave; I will see that you don't die; the battle is not yours but mine; because of Me, you will go out to face tomorrow. I am your power; I will help you. I have chosen you—no humiliation or shame here—I will rescue you; it will go well, I am the response to your questions; I am your strength, I have determined to do good for you; I will deal with things at the appointed time. No need to fear men, I am Alive; you will see me; I hear you, I have good news for you; I give to you; I don't give as the world gives, for I, your God, graciously give" (see Genesis 15:1; 21:17; 26:24 // Exodus 20:20 // Numbers 14:9 // Deuteronomy 1:17; 7:18; 31:6, 8 // Judges 6:23 // 2 Chronicles 20:15,

17; 32:7 // Isaiah 41:14; 44:8; 54:4 // Jeremiah 1:8; 40:9 // Daniel 10:2, 19 // Zachariah 8:13, 15 // Matthew 10:26, 28; 28:5, 10 //Luke 1:30; 2:10; 12:32 // John 14:27 // Acts 27:24).

A Journal Entry: Remaining in Love

We have come to know and have believed the love which God has for us. God is love, and the one who remains in love remains in God, and God remains in him.

— 1 John 4:16 (NASB)

To rely on the love God has for me means I need to live by it. I must allow the truth of love to guide me in everything. What would it mean for me to live by the truth of God's love?

It would mean that I value my life, not wishing myself harm. I would be quick to acknowledge my sins and weaknesses. I would ask for mercy more often. Before anyone else, I would first address God with my problems. I would look for answers in God rather than myself.

I would freely share with Him my disappointments and anger without self-censoring. I would embrace my humanity fully—my faults (but not exactly accept them) and all of my personality. I would be quick to listen and slow to speak. I don't have to know everything. I would be more creative, eat ice cream more regularly and not feel guilty. I would hope in the good will of the Father instead of my circumstances. I would trust my feelings less and listen to God more. Perhaps more naps would be in order, giving pause throughout the day, enjoying the little things like listening to the birds, or looking at the sky. I might see it less childish to rest in a green patch of grass and name clouds by their appearance. Crying to music would be normal, not the exception, even dancing in store aisles and be glad I got caught. I would cry more and certainly laugh more. I would care less what people do or don't do for me. I would go with less, and focus on my breathing more. Reaching out to others would be my first reaction, and I would shrink back less when I'm hurt. I would talk softer and sweeter, speak blessings, not curses. I would have fewer expectations and more hopes. I would be free to taste without indulging to be satisfied, eating less and more slowly. I would slow down and enjoy my walk to the market. Give more and keep less. I would hug more. And pet my dog more. Seeing God's might in everything would be standard practice. I would stop thinking about others, their problems, and their sins against me and think about God's plan and creation.

20 Made Alive

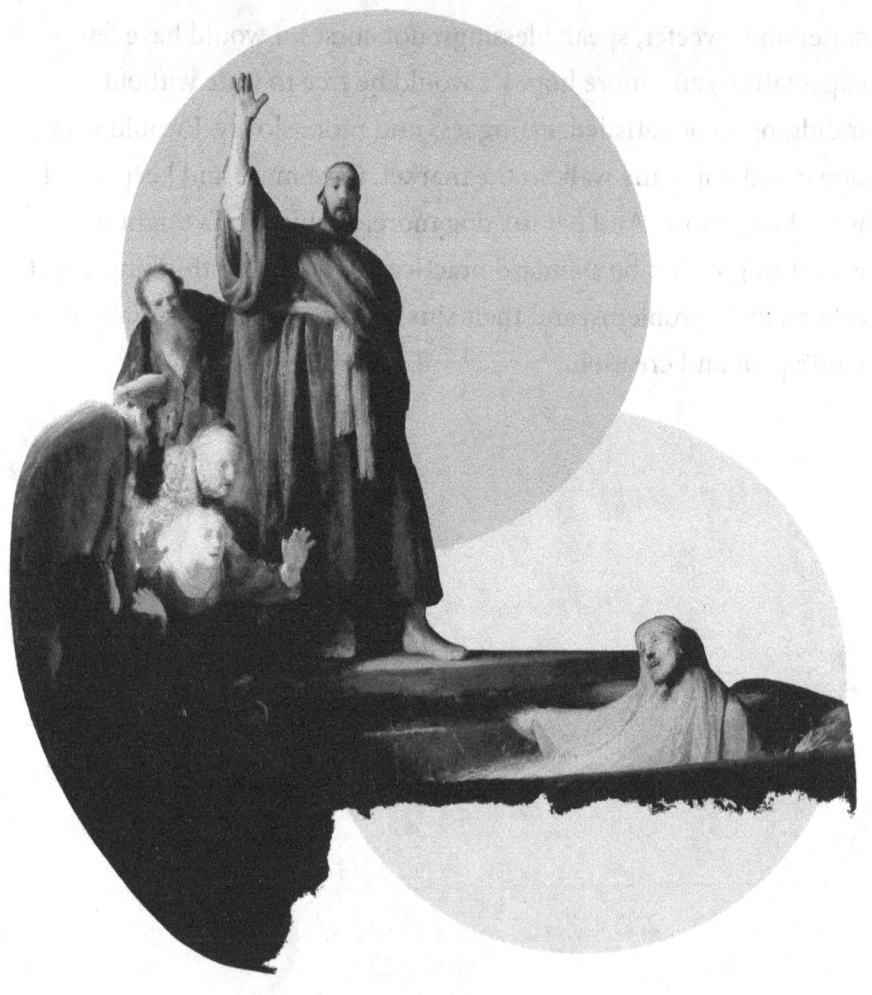

Figure 20: *Awakening*

> *God, being rich in mercy, because of the great love with which he loved us, even when we were dead in our trespasses, made us alive together with Christ...*
>
> — **Ephesians 2:4-5**

> *Do you not know that all of us who have been baptized into Christ Jesus were baptized into his death? We were buried therefore with him by baptism into death, in order that, just as Christ was raised from the dead by the glory of the Father, we too might walk in newness of life. For if we have been united with him in a death like his, we shall certainly be united with him in a resurrection like his... Now if we have died with Christ, we believe that we will also live with him.*
>
> — **Romans 6:3-5, 8**

> *For your Maker is your husband...*
>
> — **Isaiah 54:5**

There's no better way to transform than to die to an old identity and way of life and then be resurrected. Apostle Paul tells us this event happens on the occasion of baptism. This event of being lowered into the water and being lifted back out resembles burial and resurrection, and Paul says it's us sharing in the historical event of Christ's burial and resurrection. This picture of being buried and resurrected does not scream, "This is marriage!" But this is what Paul is communicating to us. We are united with Christ in this event—as a bride does on her wedding day to attach herself to the sole identity of the groom. Entering a close relationship with God is identified as marriage—the most intimate relationship one could ever have. "There comes a time in the wedding service when the bride and groom face each other," writes Welch, "it is a moment… the bride and groom are turning away from all others and have eyes for each other alone."[1] Face to face stands the couple. Spiritually, when we seek God's face (see 2 Chronicles 7:14), we turn from a life of sin, our nothingness, and allegiances to every voice and identity not of God, to face our Maker and Husband. Our Husband turns His face towards us in commitment to love us, as long as we live under His roof. Welch elaborates:

> …*this turn is a loaded action that means "I do," leaving our allegiances to choose God—there is no one else for us. The bride is now made glorious because of her husband, sharing in his holiness. She has died to shame, as shame was associated with another life, another person.*[2]

The Christian life, through Christ, is not simply "Heavenly Father, forgive me. I know exactly what I am doing wrong." It's not God emptying your bucket of sin, and then you go back into the world to fill it up again. That would be a futile life. Neither is it restricted to, "One day I'll go to Heaven, but in the meanwhile, I'll put up with my poor self." No. When you read the letters of Paul, he's saying, "No, the Christian life isn't simply about doing the best you can, knowing that you're disappointing God on an hourly basis and trying to get your sins forgiven and go to Heaven when you die."

There's way more to life than that. And that's good news. You can live a free and meaningful life. That's what Paul discusses in the letter to the Roman Christians:

> *For if we have been united with him in a death like his, we shall certainly be united with him in a resurrection like his. We know that our old self was crucified with him in order that the body of sin might be brought to nothing, so that we would no longer be enslaved to sin. For one who has died has been set free from sin. Now if we have died with Christ, we believe that we will also live with him* (Romans 6:5-8).

No one else discusses this freedom we have as Christians in the way Paul does. Here's why we should listen to him. He's been where we've been. He went from living a life enslaved to a list of dos and don'ts as a religious person who thought he found what he could do, say, read, or feel, to becoming the person he wanted to be. Paul is clear. His transformation didn't come from what he did. As we discovered in chapter one, Paul wrote a reflection about his struggle with sin as a religious person before he found the solution:

> *We know that the Law is spiritual; but I am unspiritual, sold as a slave to sin… I do not understand [approve of] what I do. For what I want to do I do not do, but what I hate I do. And if I do what I do not want to do, I agree that the Law is good. As it is, it is no longer I myself who do it, but it is sin living in me. For I know that good itself does not dwell in me, that is, in my sinful nature. For I have the desire to do what is good, but I cannot carry it out. For I do not do the good I want to*

> do, but the evil I do not want to do—this I keep on doing… Although I want to do good, evil is right there with me…What a wretched man I am! Who will rescue me from this body that is subject to death? Thanks be to God, who delivers me through Jesus Christ our Lord! So then, I myself serve the Law of God with my mind, but with my flesh I serve the Law of sin (Romans 7:14-25 NIV).

His last sentence describes our new life as Christians: "Although I lived from an outward form of human nature that lacks the willpower to live by the list of dos and don'ts—and thus imperfect—I now live in a new attitude, a new spirit of being. There's a new way of approaching life: to be about the Father's will, His business. That's my transformation."

Jesus plus nothing is the basis of our transformation.[3] Elsewhere, in Romans 5, Paul describes how we were weak imbeciles living in pig filth. It wasn't until Christ's death that we became equipped to end a life lived enslaved (verse 6). Paul goes on to explain all of it in this incredible way:

> Therefore, just as sin came into the world through one man [Adam's sinning], and death through sin, and so death spread to all men because all sinned—for sin indeed was in the world before the Law was given, but sin is not counted where there is no law. Yet death reigned from Adam to Moses, even over those whose sinning was not like the transgression of Adam, who was a type of the one who was to come. But the free gift is not like the trespass. For if many died through one

> man's [Adam's] trespass, much more have the grace of
> God and the free gift by the grace of that one man Jesus
> Christ abounded for many. And the free gift is not like
> the result of that one man's sin. For the judgment
> following one trespass brought condemnation, but the
> free gift following many trespasses brought justification.
> For if, because of one man's trespass, death reigned
> through that one man, much more will those who
> receive the abundance of grace and the free gift of
> righteousness reign in life through the one man Jesus
> Christ (Romans 5:12-17).

The entire human race was in Adam. Everybody was born into Adam. Because he was the first person, he represented us. You were Adam. And what was true of Adam became true of you. Adam sinned, and sin entered the world like a disease. Now what's so very important to see here is Paul talking about sin as if it's a thing.

It's going to be essential to understand this. Sin entered the world through Adam. When Adam sinned, it was as if all of us sinned, and we came into this world with the shame that comes with Sin, the condemnation of Sin. Sin has a domain, and you're in it. The fact is sin rules over us. We must understand how Paul doesn't just describe sin as an activity but as a thing that results in actions. There's Sin that results in sinning. One of the reasons you've not been able to change into the person you desire to be is that you have addressed the wrong you've done as mere actions. But you've never dealt with Sin, the thing, because perhaps you never realized it needed to be dealt with.

And Paul says, "The reason you keep doing things you don't want to do—the reason there's an internal battle inside of you—is because Sin lives in you. Sin is your master, and at times it's as if you have no option but to obey the Sin in you." So he says Sin—a virus and a power—entered the world through one man. And death through sin, that is, on the heels of Sin was death. Now, you've experienced this because if you have a nasty habit, you've seen the death that follows it. You killed a relationship, killed your finances, killed a career, killed something with your parents, and maybe somebody was physically killed or injured because of your sin.

Paul says that wherever sin goes, death is right behind it. The reason you know you're ungodly—the reason you learn you're sick—is the fact that you're dying. Adam sinned, and Sin entered the world like a disease. And because we're all in Adam, at some point, we became sinners too. Everybody has sinned (see Romans 3:23).

Everyone born in Adam lives in a world marked by the power and consequence of Sin—everyone born is slated to die a physical death. The world became an environment of disease, physically but also spiritually. The term "disease" comes from Middle English, meaning "lack of ease." The world post-Adam became an environment that lacked comfort, peace, and order. So as we live, we feel the lack of ease or stability in our lives—because we live in Adam. That's the bad news we've been living in. But the good news is far better than the bad news will ever be.

Paul tells us that there's a gift for us. This gift is not like what followed after the one act of Adam in the Garden that condemned all people to death. This gift is different than the trespass. If we all died because of the one trespass of the one man, then the one act of God

—through Jesus Christ—gave us the gift of life by His grace to us. Just like you were born into Adam and were placed in Adam, you may now be taken out of Adam and placed into Christ.

Notice how Paul doesn't mention anything about heaven or hell? None of that stuff is in the discussion because Paul's audience is people who are wondering, "Why can't I do what I ought to do and why does it seem that there's a thing in me, a power, that overrides my will? I know I will have regrets, wishing I hadn't done it, but I do it anyway. Is there a way to escape that?" Paul says that the gift of a "right standing" with God not only serves death a "reverse card" in a game of UNO but gives us a whole new identity. It's exciting! God's gift of grace—as opposed to the Law that sentences us to death—gives us abundant life. It's why Jesus, the one who died the death we could not die—dying to Sin as a taskmaster—says of Himself: "The thief comes only to steal, kill and, destroy. I came that they may have life and have it abundantly" (John 10:10).

The gift of abundant life has brought our justification. Justification means that when we're taken out of Adam and placed into Christ; we're given the gift of right standing before God. If you grew up in church, you might say, "That means we go to heaven when we die." And Paul would say, "That's not what I'm talking about."

Well, what are we talking about? It's more practical than that. Going to heaven when you die—that's someday. But we're talking about how it changes the dilemmas of life (i.e. – "I just can't do what I ought to do, and I can't do what the Law wants me to do. I can't please God, my mama, not even myself. I'm not consistent, and it's because this thing lives in me").

But I have some great news. The meaning of moving from Adam into Christ isn't just what happens at your death, but it's about newness in the way of living—a lifestyle here, right now. We might say, "You're not going to tell me just to try harder, are you?" No. Because this isn't about what you've tried. It's about what has become true of you.

Just as Adam did something wrong and affected everyone—they became sinners—Jesus did right and has undone what Adam did, plus made us righteous. We receive God's righteousness reign in life. There are massive implications when we think about and accept what God has done through Christ. When we're being taken out of Adam into Christ at baptism, something happens to us fundamentally. Unfortunately, maybe no one told us because it's complicated, and we don't have long attention spans. If someone did tell us, we've likely forgotten because our natural response is, "God, thank You for what You have done for me. Now I am going to live a better life." (And all the Jewish converts like Paul say, "Good luck with that!")

I'm telling you, there's been a change at the core of who you are. Your identity is now in being a beloved son or daughter of God. You have a new home, and there's a different reign you live underneath as the Bride of Christ.

Staying Dead

You can see that being made in the image of God is your true self-image. We can't allow tradition, secular distortions, or anything else to keep us away from all the truth of God's Word. Otherwise, we will never reach being free in Christ. We must understand what it means to live as a child and not as a slave.

We can't live the perfect life, but Christ can. And if Christ is our life, since we are unified with Him, we need to learn how to live life to allow Christ to live life through us. It's the art of staying dead to sin, something that Paul describes in Romans 6:

> *We know that our old self was crucified with him in order that the body of sin might be brought to nothing, so that we would no longer be enslaved to sin. For one who has died has been set free from sin. Now if we have died with Christ, we believe that we will also live with him. We know that Christ, being raised from the dead, will never die again; death no longer has dominion over him. For the death he died he died to sin, once for all, but the life he lives he lives to God. So you also must consider yourselves dead to sin and alive to God in Christ Jesus. Let not sin therefore reign in your mortal body, to make you obey its passions. Do not present your members to sin as instruments for unrighteousness, but present yourselves to God as those who have been brought from death to life, and your members to God as instruments for righteousness. For sin will have no dominion over you, since you are not under Law but under grace* (Romans 6:6-14).

Sin is not just a bad habit. It's a thing, an entity. When we struggle with temptation—voices of the world calling out—you and I aren't just wrestling with a desire, but a thing—Sin. When you're a Christian, you're taken out of Adam into Christ. What's true about life in Adam was how we became enslaved. There, our bodies became tools to do Sin's work—being both alive to Sin and associated with shame.

What is true about life in Christ is how we're children, liberated from slavery, who can now participate in Kingdom Life. It's why there's forgiveness, and why there's a life to live with the Father, who is all Goodness. See, if Sin doesn't have to control where you go when you die, Sin doesn't have to control what you do while you live. Sin is not your master. The voices of the world calling out to you is Sin trying to rule, overpower you, and enslave you to death. Why would you embrace something that would hurt you? You've died to Sin, in Christ. You've had enough death in life. Why would you live in it any longer? The power of Sin is broken, so don't let it rule you. But how?

Paul says to consider ourselves dead. The actual word Paul uses here is "to count, to reconcile" to "put it to one's account." It's an accounting term. We're to count ourselves as dead to Sin. As you accept and believe this, you need to apply this. How then is someone to occupy themselves with making such a calculation? By *declaring*.

I like how Michael Scott uses the term declare within the American comedy television series *The Office*. After a friend moves in during the episode "Money," it forces Michael to make some costly changes in life. An employee advises Michael to declare bankruptcy: "Listen, I got the answer. You declare bankruptcy, and all your problems go away." So Michael does, but not in the proper way. He walks into the office and shouts, "I. Declare. Bankruptcy!"

When Sin comes knocking at your door, we need to declare bankruptcy to Sin. There's nothing in your account with Sin. And you don't owe it. "To death do we part," is applicable here. You've nothing to offer Sin because you're dead to it. So in every moment, we must declare: "Sin is not my master!"

When you're tempted, there's a battle for your soul. At that moment, you choose which side you identify with, Sin or Christ as your master. That's the choice we're constantly making. Who'll govern over you? Sin will enslave you. Christ will liberate you.

A life devoted to Sin is a life committed to behaving how you've always behaved. Paul tells us that we must say no to Sin. Ask yourself: When I wrestle with Sin, which side of the argument do I side with, meaning when you struggle, which is the "you" side? When you're wrestling with Sin, do you wrestle from the standpoint of Adam? "Well, nobody's perfect. It's my weakness. My mother had the issue. My father did it. I can't help it. Every male does it. I can't stop it." When you do that, you're arguing from that standpoint of Adam. You're discussing it from the viewpoint of Sin and have identified with Sin. You'll lose every time because you are identifying with someone you're no longer. You're not relating to Christ, the goodness of God, but Sin. So, we must not only declare, "Sin is not my master," but decide it.

Sin is not my master, so I'm not going to let it rule me. Sin is not just behavior but an attitude. Christian growth is impossible without a persistent desire to turn away from our old Adamic nature and pursue the heart of Jesus. Spiritual growth is impossible without relentless desire, day in and day out, to come out of the world and to be with God. You need to fight the urge to fulfill the flesh. Be determined to hold onto the Truth that will last. If you fight the good fight becoming more like Jesus, you'll have something that will last throughout eternity (see 1 Timothy 6:12).

Most people fight the greatest battle of their lives to get ahead in this world. But what good are popularity, prestige, and earthly goods when you're in the grave? To be persistent in being made more into the likeness of Christ, as you need to be, a genuine heart desire to be Christ-like is essential. You must know how to repent. You must listen to the voice of God and let yourself be found by Him.

I love how Paul describes this process of choosing Christ. Paul tells us that when Sin asks us to do what it wants to do by using one of our body parts, we don't go, "Sure, Sin. Here, have some." Sin will not borrow your eyes, feet, hands, etc.! Don't loan Sin anything. When we lend our hands to do Sin's bidding, we're saying, "Here you go… bring some more death!" As Paul has said, we're to say, "You can't have my mouth or my eyes because I'm free now and don't have to obey you, Sin" (cf. Matthew 5:30). Before, you didn't have an option, but now God says you have an alternative—the opportunity to live life to God, a life of freedom. And this is why we're to devote ourselves to God.

To devote ourselves to God is the dedication to a contemplative life, reminding oneself to commit self and all our members to God. It's to daily live out "I give you my feet, eyes, ears, mouth arms, hands, and mind." It's to say to the old self knocking on the door of your heart, "My hands are already on assignment. Sin is not my master. Christ is. I have the freedom to devote myself to my Father who wants to live through me." It's a new way of thinking because it's a new way of life. We'll discuss this in chapter twenty-two, but for now, know that you have a fresh start in life, you have a fantastic new self, and the liberation you've received no one can take. The death and oppression you have experienced, and your slavery to do, is over when you're united with God.

When there's liberation from slavery, acceptance offered to you, and a new start is given, it's cause for celebration indeed!

21 Engaging the Monotony With Celebration

Figure 21: *Proudly Shepards*

It was fitting to celebrate and be glad.

— Luke 15:32

He has made everything beautiful in its time. Also, he has put eternity into man's heart, yet so that he cannot find out what God has done from the beginning to the end. I perceived that there is nothing better for them than to be joyful and to do good as long as they live; also that everyone should eat and drink and take pleasure in all his toil—this is God's gift to man.

— Ecclesiastes 3:11-13

The good news of being lost and then found, going from death to life, injects gratitude in the highs and lows of our lives. Thus, joy becomes a foundational element in the Christian experience. Jesus' parable reminds us that it is always fitting to be about celebration and gladness; in fact, it's the hallmark of those who are transformed.

When I think of the monotony of life and its prevailing issues that often trample us, I think of the elder son. For those of us going about the monotony of life—agendas and responsibilities—it's easy to be like the elder son, getting lost in a recital of work and losing that childlike attitude of wonderment. We'll never see the glory, the music, and dancing, going on at Home that way. We'll never come home and experience transformation until we behold the glory of what our Father is doing before us, and join Him in it. To do so, we must forget about what we do and take joy in what God is doing. This is the example of the prodigal who came home. He forgot what he once did and didn't do while in rebellion towards his father, and now joins his father in what he's taking joy in: the prodigal is home, and there's kingdom life to be lived. Like the prodigal's, our daily lives are transformed from moments of shame to moments of celebration in liberation from our past.

In Dr. Luke's gospel account, the birth of Jesus highlights how there's a cause for celebration within the monotony of life and why this transformative way towards living resides in it. Luke writes as a historian the narrative of Jesus being born in Bethlehem and includes the original, shocking birth announcement:

> *(8) And in the same region there were shepherds out in the field, keeping watch over their flock by night. (9) And an angel of the Lord appeared to them, and the glory of the Lord shone around them, and they were filled with great fear. (10) And the angel said to them, "Fear not, for behold, I bring you good news of great joy that will be for all the people. (11) For unto you is born this day in the city of David a Savior, who is Christ the Lord. (12) And this will be a sign for you: you will find a baby wrapped in swaddling cloths and lying in a manger." (13) And suddenly there was with the angel a multitude of the heavenly host praising God and saying, (14) "Glory to God in the highest, and on earth peace among those with whom he is pleased!" (15) When the angels went away from them into heaven, the shepherds*

> *said to one another, "Let us go over to Bethlehem and see this thing that has happened, which the Lord has made known to us." (16) And they went with haste and found Mary and Joseph, and the baby lying in a manger. (17) And when they saw it, they made known the saying that had been told them concerning this child. (18) And all who heard it wondered at what the shepherds told them. (19) But Mary treasured up all these things, pondering them in her heart. (20) And the shepherds returned, glorifying and praising God for all they had heard and seen, as it had been told them* (Luke 2:8-20).

This account is unabashedly scandalous if you wanted people to believe the story of Jesus as Christ. For there to be shepherds involved here in any way is shocking. Although the imagery of the shepherd is honorable throughout the Scriptures and used as a title for Ancient Near Eastern rulers, in the first century, you couldn't get much lower than a shepherd. Even though in almost every culture and period, the role of the shepherd was highly esteemed, literal shepherds weren't esteemed in Graeco-Roman literature. Shepherding was a despised trade.[1] Aristotle speaks negatively of the shepherd, writing:

> [that among men] the laziest are shepherds, who lead an idle life, and get their subsistence without trouble from tame animals; their flocks wandering from place to place in search of pasture; they are compelled to follow them, cultivating a sort of living farm.[2]

Aristotle seems a bit overly dramatic, doesn't he? Was it that a shepherd's daughter broke his heart as a wee lad?

Here's a bit more about shepherds. From what we know from history, shepherds could not hold public office during this period, nor was their testimony admissible as evidence in the courts.[3] To be a shepherd was forbidden occupation to the good Jew. The trade carried the greatest stigma, which resulted in the loss of civil and political rights for those who chose it, or it chose them.[4] Philo, a Hellenistic Jewish philosopher of Alexandria (the intellectual hub of that time), wrote, "There is no more disreputable occupation than that of a shepherd."[5] The first-century pious Jews had boycotted buying things from shepherds, namely wool, milk, and young sheep, because they just assumed such items were stolen.

In this time, hired shepherds would, at times, take sheep months away from the owner's property to find land upon which to graze. Unfortunately, as those sheep had offspring, there was no way to mark whether or not the flock had multiplied. So, taking the opportunity, many shepherds would steal the offspring and then sell the wool and the milk for their own—making money off their theft. Because of this, society, unfortunately, saw all shepherds as tricksters, abusers of their job who enriched themselves by dishonesty—disregarding people.[6] To be a shepherd was to be equal to the murderers, extortionists, and prostitutes.

Sadly, all those in the trade were suspected of immorality, making their public and legal life incredibly difficult. Even good shepherds would be unable to trade anything to feed their families because society would view them as thieves. Not only a thief, but a dirty vagrant and a seriously imperfect "bastard," people to be hated.[7] They were not allowed in Herod's Temple because they handled animals, and due to their supposed lifestyle, they couldn't come and worship in the temple and make a sacrifice. They were despised and rejected, wholly ostracized, and seen as wicked and depraved.

To be a shepherd was to be an expert in living a life within a string of setbacks. You went without any encounters with the glorious. You knew that you would be nothing each day. You knew how each interaction with another would go. All was predictable and unfortunate. Nothing to be anticipated and hopeful for. No reason to celebrate.

Yet, moments after the birth of Jesus, the heralding of the good news didn't go to the ruling elite. Not even to the pious, religious, or even the "average" human. But the heralding of the coming King went to those who couldn't come to God. So, therefore, God went to them, a sign of what Jesus was all about. I love this about the gospel.

What we see happening in this text is the glory of God shining around the shepherds—those who never experienced anything glorious, not even remotely. The glory of God did not shine all around those brothers waking up early in the morning to get their Torah out. Nor was it radiated to those who washed their hands ten times before their meals.* Not even those in the temple every week to seek God, nor those who made sure everyone was doing their part in society. Nope. The glory of God shone all around the shepherds, those whom society said couldn't be trusted, those whose broader culture said, "They're thieves," regardless of whether they were or not. The glory of God—the weight of God—shows up among such ones.

---

* Hand-washing was first and foremost a religious ritual that marked the difference between Jews and Gentiles until the late early modern period.

We find several incredible things in Luke 2 about what the glory of God does when it shows up. First of all, we discover that it exposes these men. Verse nine gives us a picture of them filled up to the brim with fear. The fear portrayed in the classic cartoon of Tom and Jerry comes to mind—large eyes, raised fur, hands to the chest, and legs that jump three feet. They're terrified—as if exposed to a threat. Not exactly what we would have in mind for someone's response to such an extraordinary event.

The most consistent thing people say to me in conversations about religion, or even spirituality, is that almost everybody thinks they're a good person. Everybody believes they are a good person, certainly not as bad as someone else they know. But, when the glory of God shows up, we see ourselves as who we indeed are. It exposes where we have fallen short—missed the mark. Every bit of our confidence, class, and self-justification melts in the light of His glory. The glory of God exposes all of us. It's why these brothers were terrified. I mean, sure, you could make a case that, "No, it was because it was the middle of the night, and all of a sudden, there were bright lights there." I beg to differ.

I've been in enough locker rooms and have hung out with enough men at this point in life to know that when sinful men get together, their conversations are rarely righteous. These guys in Luke 2 are most likely in the center of a field in the middle of nowhere. Nobody sees them. Nobody knows what is going on out there. We have a hard time believing that the glory of God interrupted a small Bible study—"Oh, funny that you should show up, angel! Can you help us here with Deuteronomy 7? We were just memorizing it." Hard to believe that this is what was going on when the angels interrupted. It's easier to believe it was a "Candid Camera" moment.

The glory of God exposes us for who we are. Often, we can justify that we're good and are doing great, but when the holiness of God, when the King steps in the room, all of a sudden, our confidence ebbs way, and so does the blood in our face. It's like what would happen if you played basketball against an eight-year-old. First, you would say you're great at the sport. But if Michael Jordan steps out into your court, then you're not so cocksure of yourself.

When the glory of God shows up, we are acutely made aware of our deep and desperate need for a Savior. We see this repeatedly throughout the Word of God. People who see the glory of God fall face down often. The glory of God exposes, but that's not all it does.

In verse ten, the glory of God not only exposes our darkness, but when that fear grips us, God's glory drives out fear and replaces it with joy. The purpose of wrath and judgment is to lay before us the good news that drives out fear and replaces it with joy. Look at the declaration of the angels again: "Fear not..." How is that possible? How can we not fear a holy God who is righteous, who is a just judge, who hates sin, and who rages against injustice? He is the ultimate value, measure, and standard. How am I not to fear this God of whom the most righteous in the history of the world have fallen in terror?

Well, the following declaration of the angels helps us. "Fear not..." Why? "Because I bring you good news." What is the good news that drives out the fear of our hearts about the wrath of God? Well, most know the words of John 3:16* but I'm telling you, John

---

* John 3:16 reads, "For God so loved the world, that he gave his only Son, that whoever believes in him should not perish but have eternal life."

3:17 is just as huge, if not even more. John 3:17 says, "For God did not send his Son into the world to condemn the world, but so that the world might be saved through him." When Christ shows up, Christ is coming into the dark night of the world. Jesus isn't born with a little sword and a list of people to kill for not obeying the Law. No. Christ is born as the life raft in a sea of condemnation, death, and destruction for those who will climb in to be saved from the curse present in the world. The good news is that God has made a way where we could not make way for ourselves. It's why the shepherds are getting good news.

The good news brings about great joy, but it only tends to bring about great joy in those who understand that they're sinners. If you think you're awesome, deliverance from imperfection and the shame it inflicts doesn't sound good to you because you're "awesome." If you're aware of your faults and the disgusting things you've gotten into, don't ever despise that awareness. It's such a sweet gift from God to be mindful of your shortcomings. The glory of God drives out fear and replaces it with joy because Christ came not to condemn but rather to save the world from condemnation. It's good news, and this is the Word of God.

See, when the glory of God shows up, it creates trust in the Word of God. The shepherds' reasoning in the text is stunning. They say to one another, "Let us go see this thing the Lord has made known." What I found in my heart as I was studying their response was how in our sophisticated culture, any childlike wonderment of the glory of God could fade, becoming replaced with a kind of rote routine of, "I know this is right. Let me do it." What I love about these shepherds, however, is how upon hearing the Word of the Lord from an angel, they didn't stop and go, "Did that really happen? How is that? Let's theologize about what just happened. Is God able to send angels? What do angels do? Do angels…" That's not what they did. They said, "The Lord revealed it; let's go see it!" This childlike wonderment builds confidence in what God said, which is now driving them to see what God has said would be waiting for them.

Don't we yearn for our lives to be marked by that? When I read in the Word of God that generosity changes the inner man and that generosity pleases the heart of God, I want to say, "The Lord said it; let's go see it." When I read about what God calls a husband to be, where I will love my future wife like Christ loves the Church, that she will look like a well-watered vine that produces much fruit, I want to say, "The Lord said it; let's go see it." When I think about raising children and what God says happens when parents train their children, I want to say, "The Lord said it; let's go see it." When I read in the Scriptures that the arms of the Lord are not too short to save, I want there to bubble up within me confidence in the Word of God, this sense of adventure that says, "The Lord said it; let's go see it." The glory of God builds our confidence.

When you see the weight of God, the splendor of God, the might of God, you're driven into confidence that what the Word of God says is true. Now, here's what's interesting to know. If you only plow through these verses, then you won't catch all of what the Lord wants you to see. Here's what just happened. These brothers are in the middle of nowhere, and an angel said, "Here's the sign. Here's where you find baby Jesus. He's going to be wrapped in swaddling clothes, lying in a manger." Their response is, "The Lord said it; let's go see it." Now they have the long walk to Bethlehem. Then they have to find the stable. They have no idea how long it will take them to find Jesus. We have no idea how long it took. Don't miss the fact that these men, by faith, perhaps had to leave the sheep they were in charge of to find Jesus. It involved sacrifice, and there were risks. They could have lost everything to see Jesus. They could have been wounded on their way too. To move towards Jesus was an act of faith, and their faith was rewarded—they saw Deliverance and Glory wrapped in the flesh in their ordinary lives.

  Finally, when God's glory shows up, it changes the monotony of day-to-day life. After seeing Jesus and realizing the revelation given to them, the shepherds "returned, glorifying and praising God for all they had heard and seen…" The shepherds leave rejoicing, but where were they going? Back to being shepherds, back to the fields with their smelly sheep. Back to the monotony and grind. Here is what is important to note about what the glory of God does in the day-in and day-out parts of our worlds. Nothing has changed in the social standing of the shepherds. It's not all of a sudden, having heard from angels and seeing the Messiah, that their community will accept them for the first time. It's not like they can hold a more admirable job or be able to make a good living all of a sudden. They still can't be trusted in society's eyes. Their encounter with God fixed none of that.

Yet, they left rejoicing.

  Here's what the glory of God does. The glory of God injects gratitude in the highs and lows of our lives so that joy becomes a foundational element in the Christian experience. Having beheld the glory of God, we are now intimately aware of how good and gracious God has been to us, regardless of life's circumstances.

  Think about how different things are at home when you look at your spouse and are grateful for all they do and all they bring to life rather than being an expert on all they don't do and all you wish they would. How different things would be at home when you experience your physical pain as a reminder of having life given to you by God rather than being resentful, causing your spirit to wither away! Instead of reminding us of death and our powerlessness as humans made from dirt, life's nights become visitations from God and He changes the doldrums of life. We will never be the same. There's change and transformation.

To be sure, it was the shepherds' "seeing and hearing" Immanuel (literally "God with us") that broke the darkness and blandness of their lives. Beholding who Christ was—being truly God-with-them—must have jolted them out of their humdrum existence. To have knowledge that God met them where they were to give them an incredible gift during their routine night duties must have transformed their minds. No longer would they be in self-pity—reminding themselves of how dignity, rights, and freedoms are denied to them. To be sure, they would no longer feel ashamed about their shepherding, for they didn't have to wash off the daily grime to be made acceptable. They didn't feel a desire to have some grand experience or opportunity like access to Herod's Temple to have an encounter with God. After feeling the presence of God in their daily lives, perhaps scrapping dung off their dumb sheep and always looking for green pastures weren't all that bad. God was already with them in their monotonous life, grime, sweat, sheep, and all.

It's those who will do that disciplined work of "beholding" who are shaped by the glory of God and ultimately will lead lives of joy—even on their average or worst day. Apostle Paul says, "And we all, with unveiled face, beholding the glory of the Lord, are being transformed into the same image from one degree of glory to another. For this comes from the Lord who is the Spirit" (2 Corinthians 3:18). All believers in Christ who behold God's glory are being radically changed one degree at a time into that image. What image? The image of Christ. The perfect image of God and man is in Christ Jesus. We are being made more and more like Jesus, a single degree at a time. Isn't that awesome and awful at the same time? We would much rather have "30 degrees" or "180 degrees" of change in ourselves. It would be nice to have life instantly transformed in one moment, not a lifespan of slow transformation. But this isn't what we're told happens. We may ask, "Is one degree of change in life by beholding really that special?"

Well, what if you were going off course? In mathematics class, many are asked to think about an airplane taking off. The question is posed, "If you are flying, and you—as the pilot—were one degree off course, what would happen over a time period of X?" Even without doing well in math, I would know what would happen: the plane would be flying in the wrong direction altogether and may eventually crash. If you were one degree off, everybody dies—what a humbling reality! But Paul talks about changing from one degree to the next in a positive way. In our case, one degree is the trajectory that changes everything; one degree closer to Jesus changes everything!

In our microwave day and age, where we want all issues, pains, frustrations, and all our struggles to evaporate in a second, it's the Bible that says, "No, no. Behold the glory of God one degree at a time. Nothing special must happen. And God will change everything about your inner life." One degree focused on the glory of God makes all the difference to our growth.

Journal Entry: Celebrate God All Day

Let me celebrate God all day, every day. Enjoy His presence. Don't worry; instead, pray. Before I know it, a sense of God's wholeness, everything coming together for good, will come and settle me down. Meditate on things that are true, noble, reputable, authentic, compelling, and gracious. Think of the best God has for you, and not the world's worst. Focus on the beauty shown by God and not the horror so prevalent in my world. Do this, and God, who makes everything work together for my good, will work me into His most excellent harmony of creation.

Maybe then, I'll learn to be content in whatever my circumstances are. Be happy with little as with much, and with much as with little. Be filled whether full or hungry. Whatever I have, wherever I go, I can make it through in Christ. In the mundane, I'll find beauty because I will be about God's glorious business.

I'll have to behold in meditation, with great appreciation, the love God has for me. I am being called to reach out in faith to grasp the extravagant dimensions of Christ's love. Reach out and touch love. Experience the breadth of love. Plummet to its depths. Rise to its heights. I must know the fullness of Christ's love.

I will pray for the Spirit's power to strengthen my inner being, not by my works but on Christ's. It should be in my prayer that I grow in love, not in flashy performance. May I experience the large dimensions of Christ's love and not live in the limits of an intellectual pursuit! May I only trust in God's love to perfect me, and may my adoration for God only compel me.

22 If There's Anything To Do, Then Sit

Figure 22: *Please Be Seated*

> *Look... I never disobeyed your command,*
> *yet you never gave me a [party].*
>
> *Son, you are always with me, and all that is mine is yours.*
>
> — **Luke 15:29 & 32**

Whose fault was it that the elder son went without rest and joy as a son? That was my first thought reading the parable's end. That's the wrong question though, isn't it? Looking at the parable, we see how our relationship with our Father is based on being with Him, unlike the world's performance mandate. But somehow, there are those like the elder son and me, whose performance-based society has conditioned them into thinking that living perfectly–conquering every bad habit and doing good works for merit–enables us to enjoy the blessings of a relationship with the Father, like joy and mercies. "These many years I've been slaving away for you... I never disobeyed your command. And it's about time for me to sit down as your heir and celebrate!" To receive good gifts from the Father, we rate our daily performance to see if we merit His mercies, such as a celebratory victorious life.

Like the elder son, however, we've been made heirs of His kingdom's riches all this time as Christians, but we've often forfeited them, thinking we had to prove ourselves capable of reigning victoriously. We must know that the good works we do, don't imply that we are walking right with God, even though good works must always accompany us in kingdom life as His heirs. Just look at the elder brother's condescending attitude and his detachment from his father's work at home by being attached to his own!

Warning against such a faithless life, Paul cautions us against such people who don't hold fast to the Christ, the "Head, from whom the whole body, nourished and knit together through its joints and ligaments, grows with a growth that is from God" (Colossians 2:19). Paul writes:

> *If with Christ you died to the elemental spirits of the world, why, as if you were still alive in the world, do you submit to regulations— "Do not handle, Do not taste, Do not touch" (referring to things that all perish as they are used)—according to human precepts and teachings? These have, indeed, an appearance of wisdom in promoting self-made religion and asceticism and severity to the body, but they are of no value in stopping the indulgence of the flesh* (Colossians 2:20-23).

Paul's point: Attachment to human religion is detachment from Christ.

Typically, there's a list either perceived by the new Christian or a list given by the older Christian. It's often on a restrictive basis and is generally negative—full of don'ts. To live by the list of human regulations and traditions is often misunderstood as living the spiritual life—a life at home. But it's not true. As Francis Schaeffer attests, "The true Christian life, true spirituality, is not merely a negative not-doing of any small list of things."[1] Even if there are lists needed to walk appropriately within the world as Christians (see

Romans 4; Acts 16:1-5, and Acts 15 [specifically verses 22-29]), we must still know that the importance of the true Christian life is not only the avoidance of external defilement (Matthew 23:27). Life with the Father neither begins nor is maintained by minding what to be against only but for (practically speaking). Because, naturally, when we choose certain things, we also decide to leave other things to find them (see Matthew 13:44-46).

To help us live as true Children of God about His work, Apostle Paul gives us an incredible insight into this ordinary Christian life. It's not only insightful but crucial to understanding such a life. If it were not, Paul wouldn't have repeated it in his letter to the Ephesians:

> ...*the God of our Lord Jesus Christ... raised him from the dead and seated him at his right hand in the heavenly places, far above all rule and authority and power and dominion, and above every name that is named, not only in this age but also in the one to come* (Ephesians 1:20-21).

> ... *and raised us up with him and seated us with him in the heavenly places in Christ Jesus, so that in the coming ages he might show the immeasurable riches of his grace in kindness toward us in Christ Jesus. For by grace you have been saved through faith. And this is not your own doing; it is the gift of God, not a result of works, so that no one may boast* (Ephesians 2:6-9).

The message is clear: God made Christ sit and made us sit with Him. The Christian life does not begin until we sit with Him, just as the Christian birth does not happen until one dies and becomes resurrected. To be raised is also to be seated. Through faith in Christ, by His grace, we have died, been raised to new life, and now are seated. The word "sit" reveals the true beginning of our Christian experience.

Sitting is hard because our fleshly nature does not understand life and value or progress with its involvement. Naturally, it protests. On top of that, most Christians make the mistake of trying to walk a Christian walk by themselves to sit with Christ—a holy and honored place. That is to say, people live as if there's a need to try to deserve the title Christian and the liberated life under Christ. But that is a reversal of God's order. Watchman Nee explains that "Our natural reason says, *If we do not walk, how can we ever reach the goal? What can we attain without effort? How can we ever get anywhere if we do not move?*"[2] We are like toddlers, squirming in our seats, anxious and troubled. But if anyone had parents, we know that hanging halfway off your chair is not considered sitting at all.

As Nee sharply observes:

If at the outset we try to do anything, we get nothing; if we seek to attain something, we miss everything. For Christianity begins not with a big do, but with a big done... We began our Christian life by depending not upon our own doing, but upon what He had done.[3]

Once seated, and only when we are seated, may we reign victoriously, sharing in Christ's victory over Sin and death, that is, to live the Christian life Paul lays out in his letter to the Colossians:

If then you have been raised with Christ, seek the things that are above, where Christ is, seated at the right hand of God. Set your minds on things that are above, not on things that are on earth. For you have died, and your life is hidden with Christ in God. When Christ who is your life appears, then you also will appear with him in glory.

Put to death therefore what is earthly in you: sexual immorality, impurity, passion, evil desire, and covetousness, which is idolatry. On account of these the wrath of God is coming. In these you too once walked, when you were living in them. But now you must put them all away: anger, wrath, malice, slander, and obscene talk from your mouth. Do not lie to one another, seeing that you have put off the old self with its practices and have put on the new self, which is being renewed in knowledge after the image of its creator...

Put on then, as God's chosen ones, holy and beloved, compassionate hearts, kindness, humility, meekness, and patience, bearing with one another and, if one has a complaint against another, forgiving each other; as the Lord has forgiven you, so you also must forgive. And above all these put on love, which binds everything together in perfect harmony... And whatever you do, in word or deed, do everything in the name of the Lord Jesus, giving thanks to God the Father through him (Colossians 3:1-10, 12-14, 17).

Apostle Paul's first directive to those new or old in Christ, or to the prodigals and the elders, isn't to keep a checklist. Instead, our instruction is to "seek the things that are above." The Greek meaning is "to have a mind for spiritual things." We can liken this to the expression, "It has a mind of its own." This kind of will and desire is what Paul has in mind. It's an attitude of the heart, where all you desire before anything else is the Kingdom of God (see Matthew 6:33). Your sole delight—your highest satisfaction—in life is being about and sharing in the Father's business because His work is exciting and honorable, in one word: sanctification (see James 2:14-26 and 1 Thessalonians 5:22-24).

It is saying that we have not done anything to be able to reign with Christ in the heavenly realms, yet we share His power and kingdom through faith by God's grace. Once seated, with Christ as the beloved, we'll walk in Him as commanded in the Letter to the Colossians. After all, faith without works is dead, and faith in the Christian life does not save, but obedience to the grace of God (see James 2:14-26).

If one is concerned about their inability to begin to reign victoriously in life as described by Paul's list of new attitudes, be comforted: Paul says the Christian's ability to reign over Sin in this life is available because we live no longer as ourselves, but Christ, the victor, becomes our life.

As we are sitting in Christ, we will, too, walk in Him and His ways.

It's why in his letter to the Ephesians, Paul opens with the statement that God has blessed us in Christ "with every spiritual blessing in the heavenly places" (Ephesians 1:3). So at the very start, we are invited to sit down and enjoy what God has done for us. There is no invitation to set out to try and achieve for ourselves, for God says that we are saved, not by works, but "by grace… through faith" (Ephesians 2:8). And if your salvation is not of your own doing—that it is not a result of your works—but a gift, indeed you will walk a Christian life by God's work, not as the result of your efforts alone. It's also why we are told, "For we are his workmanship, created in Christ Jesus for good works, which God prepared beforehand, that we should walk in them" (Ephesians 2:10). We are Christ's workmanship, and we share in His work and walk. Therefore, "The Christian life from start to finish is based upon" one truth: complete dependence on Christ.[4] The only way we make progress in the Christian life is first by sitting down, being His workmanship, and then diving into the work God shares with us, walking in the ways of Christ by faith.

The Successful Life

Success is not measured, not at least in the way that the world measures. It's not in the number of people you impacted, nor how many times you added to someone's value in life. (However, such things are good works that naturally flow out of our partnership with God because that is true Christian life.) Success is measured by how much you allowed the Presence of God to conform you to the image of Jesus, the perfect image of a human walking and working with God, to live out your salvation. It is as George Morrison states in his book *If It's Not Broken, Break it!*, "The Christian walk is not a one-time experience but an ongoing way of life… Fellowship only begins with the establishment of a Father-child relationship; then it must move into a day-to-day communion, as you get to know the Father, Son, and Holy Spirit."[5] Personal spiritual growth is of utmost importance, as it is the way of your transformation and the transformation of others that you lead (see James 1:27 and Ephesians 4). We're talking about maturity leading to the building up the body of Christ, until our unity as God's family is "to the measure of the stature of the fullness of Christ" (Ephesians 4:13).

Many Christians anxiously obsess over their weaknesses, thinking that all would be OK if only they were better or stronger. The idea that failure to live a perfect life by ourselves alone is due to not trying hard enough naturally leads to this false idea of deliverance.[6] Nee tells us that if we are obsessed "with the power of sin and with our inability to meet it, then we naturally conclude that to gain the victory over sin we must have more power."[7] If our way of being with Christ started with "Lord, thank You for dying the death I could not die," why do we now say, "Lord, help me exercise more willpower to live the life I can't live"? Doing more or having more willpower is not Christianity. Nee adequately assesses our misunderstanding:

> *God's way of delivering us from sin is not by making us stronger and stronger but by making us weaker and weaker. That is indeed a rather peculiar way of victory, you say, but it is the Divine way. God sets us free from the dominion of sin, not by strengthening our old man but by crucifying him; not by helping him to do anything but by removing him from the scene of action.*[8]

So, what is a victorious Christian life? If living as an overcomer has nothing to do with what I do, in the sense of doing as myself, not in Christ, what does it have to do with? There is no indication within the New Testament that we must do anything other than be with Christ to be made right and productive. The reason I know this is how Jesus doesn't tell us to be "successful" but to be fruitful:

> *I am the vine; you are the branches. Whoever abides in me and I in him, it is he that bears much fruit, for apart from me you can do nothing. If anyone does not abide in me he is thrown away like a branch and withers; and the branches are gathered, thrown into the fire, and burned. If you abide in me, and my words abide in you, ask whatever you wish, and it will be done for you. By this, my Father is glorified, that you bear much fruit and so prove to be my disciples* (John 15:5-8).

A tree does not stress all day about being a tree, and a good tree is that. Neither does it worry and work hard to pop out its fruit. Apostle Paul tells us in his letter to the churches in Galatia that the fruit or the product of those who remain attached to the Vine are "love, joy, peace, patience, kindness, goodness, faithfulness, gentleness, self-control; against such things, there is no law" (Galatians 5:22-23). Given this truth, our being with or remaining attached to Christ is essential to producing everything good. And growing into everything good is the essence of transformation. Not choosing to be with ends all productivity and goodness. It's why so many people who have chosen against being with have failed and failed society.

Journal Entry: I Worked More

For the kingdom of heaven is like a master of a house who went out early in the morning to hire laborers for his vineyard. After agreeing with the laborers for a denarius a day, he sent them into his vineyard. And going out about the third hour, he saw others standing idle in the marketplace, and to them, he said, "You go into the vineyard too, and whatever is right I will give you." So they went. Going out again about the sixth hour and the ninth hour, he did the same. And about the eleventh hour he went out and found others standing. And he said to them, "Why do you stand here idle all day?" They said to him, "Because no one has hired us." He said to them, "You go into the vineyard too." And when evening came, the owner of the vineyard said to his foreman, "Call the laborers and pay them their wages, beginning with the last, up to the first." And when those hired about the eleventh hour came, each of them received a denarius. Now when those hired first came, they thought they would receive more, but each of them also received a denarius. And on receiving it they grumbled at the master of the house, saying, "These last worked only one hour, and you have made them equal to us who have borne the burden of the day and the scorching heat." But he replied to one of them, "Friend, I am doing you no wrong. Did you not agree with me for a denarius? Take what belongs to you and go. I choose to give to this last worker as I give to you. Am I not allowed to do what I choose with what belongs to me? Or do you begrudge my generosity?" So the last will be first, and the first last.

— Matthew 20:1-16

My Feelings As The First Hired:

I deserve more because I have worked more than those who just now began to work. Why should they be equal to me? I have been slaving away here. They nearly broke a sweat today!

My Feelings As The Last Hired:

Don't the first hired deserve more? They worked more and received the same. I don't deserve to be equal.

Also, As The Last Hired:

I'm delighted to be treated with compassion. I am excited to be honored the same as everyone else who has more work to show. I am grateful to my boss—feeling indebted to him. He seems to care. I believe that he is not harsh and doesn't expect my work to be the same as others, but will nevertheless treat me with the same dignity. I feel that the boss is not as gracious to those who have worked—they're getting paid the same as me but for more work. It seems unfair to them. It's upside down. But I am grateful for the favor, and the boss can do what he pleases. Plus, he hasn't broken any promises. We all got what the contract stated, though I received more than expected, and the others received what they expected.

My Conclusion:

The difference in our responses lies in expectations. On the one hand, we may be ungrateful and resentful for what was promised and what we received. On the other hand, we are thankful for what was given, despite how we feel about our work input. The first group of laborers worked all of the time. The second group worked some of the time. For the boss to give more to a worker who just started at the end of the day, then pay equally the group working all day is odd. The second group's work is not equal to the first's. But the boss paid out the same as if it was equal to them. "I thought we should be paid according to our work and not paid for just being in the field." Favoritism? No, both groups received the same because the promises were the same for both.

    I identify with the last batch of workers brought into the field. I have not kept the regulations, the sacrifices, the cleaning practices that the Israelites kept in the Old Testament, but I enjoy my freedom. I wasn't even looking for salvation when offered to me. I put in no effort but trust. It changes the ballgame. It's about with not do.

Conclusion:
With Is Greater Than *Do*

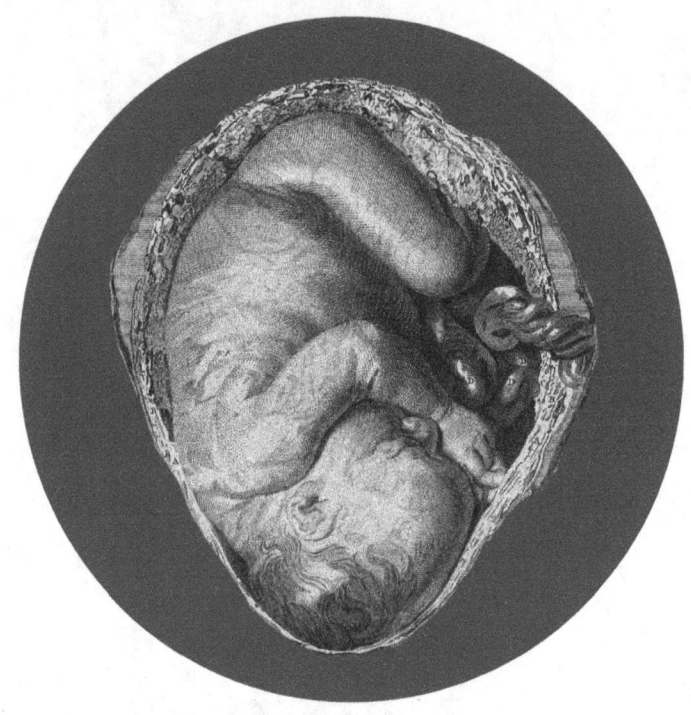

Figure 23: *Rebirth*

You've just crossed the finish line of this book, and your head and heart are filled with the good news that you can be the person you want to be. We've lived together through the journeys presented in this book, but you know there's a journey of your own to live. You're probably wondering, *Where do I begin?*

I suggest you start by finding where you are in your journey toward becoming a child that belongs—someone who accepts their acceptance by choosing to be instead of do. The parable of *The Prodigal Son* gives us two people we can identify with. We can see ourselves in them by their choices, and let their choices reveal to us where transformation lies for an abundant life. By doing this, we will know where we came from, where we are, and where we are heading—three things can lead us to be the person we want to be. With our new knowledge of how being with is greater than doing, we can make sure we're headed for an abundant life.

For many of us, life has been reduced to what rules and expectations we met. Performing well has meant that life will go well for you—filled with meaning and value. We have relied on flawless performance to gain our well-being—belonging, acceptance. No wonder people struggle with having imperfections. Knowing that we're imperfect in a world that gives us value according to our performance has led us to live meaningless lives. When life begins to crack, and those embarrassing flaws threaten to reveal our imperfect selves, life appears to be void of meaning. We scramble to rearrange our lives to appear good enough, to meet expectations—hiding behind our masks. Everyone may like us, but nobody will know us. No wonder we live insufferable lives that lack intimate relationships, intense meaning, and transformative faith!

In this book, we've challenged work-based acceptability to find value and meaning in our lives. And we've found that being is greater than doing when inside a relationship with God—the Author of life. Our relationship with God never begins with what we do for God, nor will it be sustained by what we do. It always starts with what God has done for us and never ends with what we have done, as long as we return home to Him. If we internalized this truth and made this the core reality of our being, we would stand utterly transformed and indistinguishable from our source, set aglow, and forever freed. If you get this from your head to your heart, it will impact every part of your life—fulfillment lies in ending our love affair with slavery and living out of pure being.

My struggle with do led to my encounter with death that made me challenge the system of doing and my reliance on it for happiness. Being a Christian with education and training in the Bible, I naturally turned there for answers to my life's problem: *Why couldn't I live as the person I wanted to be?* Having faith in Christ's Word on how the Christian life is different than life in the world as a life of abundance, I knew I'd missed something because I wasn't experiencing it. So I set out to look at Scripture. From my findings, especially in Christ's parable of *The Prodigal Son*, I suggest that if we learned to replace do-ness with is-ness, then we would be able to live abundant lives, free from the chains of a deep sense of unworthiness. The big discovery was how our value doesn't come from what we do. That wholeness in life isn't found in our performance but in relationship. We can discover belonging and value apart from the struggle for flawless performance. When we began this book together, I promised that if we ended our obsession with performance, we'd transform our sense of self that will create meaning and value in life.

When we realize that there is no substance in the things we do and that we are objectified in them, we start to accept that doing will never be the way to our well-being. Out of self-preservation, we change our attitude towards what doing can do for us, accepting the gift of unconditional acceptance—a foundation for everything that lives and grows.

We saw how natural it is for us as humans to think about how our value is in measure of our performance. What we think about ourselves and what people and the culture think about us normally revolve around what we do. And that's why, no matter where you go, people exist in one of two groups: rule-keepers and rule-breakers. So doing was the way to well-being when we belonged to the first group. The systems of do inherently promised to bring about wholeness in us because we felt there was something wrong with us. But we see how they make no one perfect. They only exposed us for who we are —imperfect and unacceptable. Shame gripped our soul's core. When contempt is felt from your community because of what you do or fail to do, it's easy to think that God joins them. And what we believe about what God thinks when thinking about us shapes our ultimate view of ourselves. This is why, if there is any lasting relief and real transformation in this life, there will need to be a new identity given to us by God. This new identity gets us living beyond the failure of not being the people we want to be.

So, when Christ gave us the parable of *The Prodigal Son*, we realized that there is no substance in the things we do but that we become objectified in them. The parable presented a new scenario that challenged our perception of the basis for which God gives us placement and acceptance. We came to accept that doing will never be the answer to our well-being. We have changed our attitude towards what doing can do for us, accepting the gift of unconditional acceptance out of self-preservation.

Here are the set of questions to ask yourself to see where you are at in your struggle against doing for your transformation. After you conclude this book, give yourself 15 minutes to start being. Get yourself a solitary place with little to no distractions. Take paper and writing utensils with you, maybe a cup of coffee or tea. Take the first five minutes to quiet your mind, and turn your attention to your body. Notice if there's any tension or pain in the body. Count the seconds in each of your breaths. Pray to the LORD, asking Him to help you become aware of the movements of your heart as you read the questions. Take another five minutes to read once or twice the list of questions on the next three pages all the way through. Afterward, answer the question(s) you felt created tension and/or excitement in you. Write down your answers. Take the last five minutes to compare your answers with the attitudes and actions of the elder son and the prodigal son in the parable. Find the character and what part of their journey represents your answer to life right now. It will give you an idea of how and where you are and where you will be for the rest of your day, reflecting how you can choose to be rather than do.

A. Are you doing everything and anything you can for well-being, being far away from intimate relationships?

B. Are you in denial that you're not able to be the person you want to be by your performance?

C. Are you gravitating towards people who don't know you and like it that way?

D. How about punishment? Do you tend to appreciate rules more than openness in relationships?

E. Do you struggle with your imperfections and feel that they are greater than the compassion you're able to receive?

F. Is God giving you the gift of acceptance right now, but you're having a hard time accepting it?

G. Is life marked by the freedom to do something or not do something?

H. Do you have open hands, ready to receive whatever comes your way?

I. Can you celebrate and delight in small things that you would otherwise dismiss as petty or even uncalled for?

J. Do you focus on what people do for you and what you do for them in your relationships? Do you keep record?

K. Do you meet every encounter in life with expectation or anticipation? (Two very different attitudes.)

L. Can you rest and be alone without having to do anything distracting or feel anxious?

Word From The Author

I'm Thomas. I'm a good hypocrite, a vagabond, and a mentally distraught codependent, saved by grace. I was a pastor and engaged, but no longer.

How I got to those places and why I left them is the story of my life.

But it's not the whole story.

"know for certain that God has made him both Lord and Christ, this Jesus whom you crucified." Now when they heard this they were cut to the heart, and said to Peter and the rest of the apostles, "Brothers, what shall we do?" And Peter said to them, "Repent and be baptized every one of you in the name of Jesus Christ for the forgiveness of your sins, and you will receive the gift of the Holy Spirit. For the promise is for you and for your children and for all who are far off, everyone whom the Lord our God calls to himself." And with many other words he bore witness and continued to exhort them, saying, "Save yourselves from this crooked generation." So those who received his word were baptized...

– **Acts 2:36-41**

When is God's grace applied to our life?

SOURCE
God's
Riches
At
Christ's
Expense

MEANS
A spiritual trust in God beyond what we can see or experience.

OCCASION
Pledge of a clear conscience towards God.
— *1 Peter 3:21*

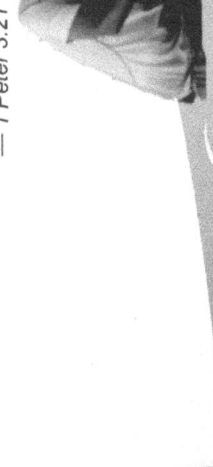

BY **GRACE** THROUGH **FAITH** AT **BAPTISM**

- "For it is **by grace** you have been saved, **through faith** and this is not from yourselves, it is the gift of God." — Ephesians 2:8
- "We were therefore **buried with him through baptism** into death. Just as Christ was raised from the dead through the glory of the Father, we too may live a new life." — Romans 6:4
- "He who has believed and has been **baptized** shall be saved." — Mark 16:16

Used by Permission. MERCYPARTNERS © 2021 www.mercy-partners.org

Acknowledgments

Tom and Sandie Kilian

My parents. Who taught me how to live life to the fullest. Tom who saved me from myself multiple times. Sandie who cared for my emotional wounds like the hand of God.

Helen Kilian

My twin sister. Who exemplifies how to celebrate life, and who shed tears when no other friend would with me.

Tom and Roberta Kilian

My grandparents. Tom Sr. who showed me proper work ethic. Roberta who taught me the importance for journaling and prayer.

Becky Hill

A spiritual director and friend who guided me to come home to myself and shared/inspired major spiritual realities now written within this book. The only one who had nothing to gain by helping me but gave freely.

Adam Henderson

My uncle in the faith. Who gave me my first Red Ryder, and didn't force empty advice on me when I was broken. He taught me about the ministry of presence.

Tina Nipper

My English professor who taught me how to write well.

Benny and Vickie Furrow

My sweet neighbors who cared for my well-being in friendship. They reminded me of home.

Walter Shelton

My dear brother in the faith who showed me the way of being an authentic human. Rest in peace, friend.

Jedidiah McCollough

My friend and classmate. Who taught me how to live under vows of poverty, chastity, and obedience.

Mrs. Pat

A friend who had a vision of paradise as a place flowing with love, but died before completing her book on it. Rest in peace, friend.

Vincent Van Gogh

A preacher and artist, but more importantly a fellow tormented soul who's artistry found God's goodness in the land of the living.

Figures

Figure 1: This work, "Hiding Our Nakedness," is a derivative of "Adam en Eva verbergen zich voor God de Vader Schepping en zondeval (serietitel) Historia creationis mundi (serietitel) Thesaurus sacrarum historiarum veteris testamenti, elegantissimis imaginibus e" (www.rijksmuseum.nl/nl/collectie/RP-P-1995-25-8), by Rijks Museum (www.rijksmuseum.nl/nl) used under CC0 BY 1.0(www.creativecommons.org/publicdomain/zero/1.0/deed.en).

Figure 2: This work, "Beholder," is a derivative of "Wonder eye" (commons.wikimedia.org/wiki/File:Wonder_eye.png) by Jalal Volker, (www.commons.wikimedia.org/wiki/User:Jalal), used under CC BY-SA 3.0 (www.creativecommons.org/licenses/by-sa/3.0/deed.en).

Figure 3. This work, "Judas Betrays Jesus", is a derivative of "Gustave Doré, Study for 'The Judas Kiss', Walters" (www.commons.wikimedia.org/wiki/File:Gustave_Doré_-_Study_for_"The_Judas_Kiss"_-_Walters_371387.jpg), by The Walters Art Museum (www.thewalters.org), used under CC BY-SA 3.0, (www.creativecommons.org/licenses/by-sa/3.0/deed.en) {{PD-US}} (www.commons.wikimedia.org/wiki/Template:PD-US).

Figure 4: This work, "God on the Cross," is a derivative of "2018901116," used under license from Shutterstock.com.

Figure 5: This work, "Judas Walking Away," is a derivative of "Judas" (www.artyzm.com/obraz.php?id=12214), by National Museum in Warsaw, (www.mnw.art.pl/en/) used under {{PD-US-expired}} (www.commons.wikimedia.org/wiki/Template:PD-US).

Figure 6: This work, "Addiction Is A Behemoth Black Hole," is a derivative of "Behemoth Black Hole Found in an Unlikely Place" (www.flickr.com/photos/24662369@N07/26209716511), by NASA Goddard Space Flight Center, (www.flickr.com/photos/gsfc/) used under CC BY 2.0 (www.creativecommons.org/licenses/by/2.0/).

Figure 7: This work, "The Prodigal's Purgatory," is a derivative of "Pierre Puvis de Chavannes The Prodigal Son c. 1879" (www.nga.gov/collection/art-object-page.46675.html), by National Gallery of Art (www.nga.gov/), used under CC0 BY 1.0 (www.creativecommons.org/publicdomain/zero/1.0/).

About the artwork: Kilian's use of De Chavannes' painting of the prodigal son captures the utter brokenness and encounter with great suffering. Naked nearly with only a wrap across his waist is likened to Christ's many portrayals on the cross. It represents who Christ is to us, God with Us sharing in our suffering and wounds. The son's arms are crossed in an embrace. He seems to be embracing himself in compassion like would a mother her child. He is almost lying in the fetal position, reminding us of the new birth which awaits him. Birth is about to take place. We then see him on the ground. He's connected to where he came, the dust, and thus realizes his morality. He's also on the ground with the pigs. In a way, he becomes like one of them while losing all human dignity.

Figure 8: This work "Burial in Baptism," is a derivative of "John Craven Performs a Baptism at Iwo Jima, 1945 (8080641690)" (www.flickr.com/photos/usmcarchives/8080641690/), by USMC Archives (www.flickr.com/photos/usmcarchives/), used under CC BY 2.0 (www.creativecommons.org/licenses/by/2.0/).

Figure 9: This work, "Athlete Derek Redmond Limping Home With Father," is a derivative of "English Track Athlete Derek Redmond of the Great Britain Team, by picture id 720889803," used under license from Gettyimages.com.

Figure 10: This work "The Tender Embrace of Forgiveness," is a derivative of "George Grey Barnard, Sir, Prodigal Son, Clemen, p.20" (www.commons.wikimedia.org/wiki/File:Barnard_Prodigal_Son_Clemen_p.20.jpg), by Paul Clemen, used under {{PD-US-expired}} (www.commons.wikimedia.org/wiki/Template:PD-US-expired).

Figure 11: This work, "The Return," is a derivative of "Return of the Prodigal Son, Rembrandt Harmensz van Rijn" (www.artsandculture.google.com/asset/5QFIEhic3owZ-A), by the The State Hermitage Museum (www.artsandculture.google.com/partner/the-state-hermitage-museum), used under CC0 BY 1.0 (www.creativecommons.org/publicdomain/zero/1.0/).

Figure 12: This work, "Peter Alerted," is a derivative of "St Peter Alerted by St John to Presence of the Lord and Casts Himself into Water, by James Tissot," by www.Restoredtraditions.com, used under CC0 BY 1.0 (www.creativecommons.org/publicdomain/zero/1.0/).

Figure 13: This work, "Home, Solace from the Desert," is a derivative of "The Houses of the Rich and Poor Man, Dives and Lazarus" (www.digitalcollections.nypl.org/items/510d47d9-5da9-a3d9-e040-e00a18064a99), by The New York Public Library(www.digitalcollections.nypl.org), used under {{PD-US-expired}} (www.commons.wikimedia.org/wiki/Template:PD-US).

Figure 14: This work, "High Priest in Holied Garments," is a derivative of "The High Priest In Garments of Glory and Beauty, by B. Scoss", by Thomas Kilian III, used under {{PD-Scan}} (www.commons.wikimedia.org/wiki/Commons:When_to_use_the_PD-scan_tag).

Figure 15: This work, "Sanctify Me," is a derivative of a photograph taken of first-century C.E. stone jars in the Collection of the IAA, The Isreal Museum in Jerusalem.

Figure 16: This work, "Irate," is a derivative of "The face of an angry man. Drawing, 18th century (?), after C. Le Brun. no. 32493i" (www.catalogue.wellcomelibrary.org/record=b1190330), by Wellcome Library (www.catalogue.wellcomelibrary.org), used under CC BY 4.0 (www.creativecommons.org/licenses/by/4.0/).

Figure 17: This work, "Father, Stretch Out Your Hand," is a derivative of "1488283709", by used under license from Shutterstock.com.

Figure 18: This work, "Time Passes By," is a derivative of "Pink rose in white background" (www.commons.wikimedia.org/wiki/File:Pink_rose_in_white_background.jpg#/media/File:Pink_rose_in_white_background.jpg), by George E. Koronaios (https://commons.wikimedia.org/wiki/User:George_E._Koronaios) used under CC BY-SA 4.0 (www.creativecommons.org/licenses/by-sa/4.0/)

Figure 19: "Child-Like" by Thomas Kilian III © 2004.

Figure 20: This work, "Awakening," is a derivative of "Rembrandt Harmensz. van Rijn - The Raising of Lazarus - Google Art Project" (www.artsandculture.google.com/asset/fQHHfdhrdSaVoA), by Los Angeles County Museum of Art (www.artsandculture.google.com/partner/los-angeles-county-museum-of-art), used under {{PD-US}} (www.commons.wikimedia.org/wiki/Template:PD-US).

Figure 21: This work, "Proudly Shepards," is a derivative of "Creative Commons Live stock: a cyclopedia for the farmer and stock owner…" (www.flickr.com/photos/internetarchivebookimages/14798293173/), by Internet Archive Book Images (www.flickr.com/photos/internetarchivebookimages/), used under CC BY 2.0 (www.creativecommons.org/licenses/by/2.0/).

Figure 22: This work, "Please Be Seated," is a derivative of "Folding Stool" (www.metmuseum.org/art/collection/search/544252), by Rogers Fund, 1912, The Metropolitan Museum (www.metmuseum.org), used under CC BY 1.0 (www.creativecommons.org/publicdomain/zero/1.0).

Figure 23: This work, "Rebirth", is a derivative of "Dissection of the pregnant uterus, showing the foetus at eight months, with the head positioned towards the vagina. Copperplate engraving by J.C. Bryer after I.V. Rymsdyk, 1774, reprinted 1851" (www.wellcomecollection.org/works/twcef6st), by Wellcome Collection (www.wellcomecollection.org), used under CC BY PDM 1.0 (www.creativecommons.org/publicdomain/mark/1.0).

Permissions

Excerpts from THE RETURN OF THE PRODIGAL SON: A STORY OF HOMECOMING by Henri Nouwen, copyright © 1992 by Henri J. M. Nouwen. Used by permission of Doubeday Religion, an imprint of Random House, a division of Penguin Random House LLC. All rights reserved.

The Furious Longing of God © 2009 by Brennan Manning. Used by permission of David C Cook. May not be further reproduced. All rights reserved.

Some content taken from *Abba's Child* by Brennan Manning. Copyright © 1994, 2002, 2015. Used by permission of NavPress, represented by Tyndale House Publishers. All rights reserved.

Notes

Chapter One – Why We Do: Nakedness and Fig Leaves

1. *A Brief History of Thought: a Philosophical Guide to Living*, by Luc Ferry and Theo Cuffe, Canongate Books Ltd, 2019.

2. *Shame Interrupted: How God Lifts the Pain of Worthlessness and Rejection*, by Edward T. Welch, New Growth Press, 2012, pp. 11–12.

3. Ibid, p. 12.

4. Ibid, pp. 15-18.

5. Ibid, p. 19.

6. Ibid, p. 8.

7. *Healing for Damaged Emotions*, by David A. Seamands, David C Cook, 2015, p. 49.

Chapter Two – In the Eye of the Beholder: Who Are You?

1. CBS. "Mike Tyson: My Belts Are Garbage." YouTube, 29 May 2011, www.youtube.com/watch?v=pgcHBcQRlpw.

Chapter Three – He Wanted Dad Dead

1. Barry, John D., editor. "Pharisee." *The Lexham Bible Dictionary*, Digital ed., Lexham Press, 2016.

2. Barry, John D., editor. "Scribe." *The Lexham Bible Dictionary*, Digital ed., Lexham Press, 2016.

3. *The Sinner in Luke*, Dwayne H. Adams, Pickwick Publications, 2008.

4. Barry, John D., editor. "Sin, the Sinner." *The Lexham Bible Dictionary*, Digital ed., Lexham Press, 2016.

5. *Poet and Peasant; and, Through Peasant Eyes: a Literary-Cultural Approach to the Parables of Luke*, by Kenneth E. Bailey, William B. Eerdmans, 1983, pp. 161–164.

6. Ibid, p. 164.

Chapter Four – God is Dead?

1. *The Return of the Prodigal Son: A Story of Homecoming*, by Henri J.M. Nouwen, Kindle ed., The Crown Publishing Group, 1994, p. 48.

2. Ibid.

3. *God Is Dead. God Remains Dead. And We Have Killed Him*, by Friedrich Wilhelm Nietzsche, et al, Kindle ed., Penguin Books, 2020, pp. 57-58.

Chapter Five – The "Indecent" Luxury of Rejection

1. *The Return of the Prodigal Son: A Story of Homecoming*, by Henri J.M. Nouwen, Kindle ed., The Crown Publishing Group, 1994, p. 59.

2. Ibid, p. 60.

3. Ibid, p. 50.

4. Ibid, p. 53.

5. *Abba's Child: The Cry of the Heart for Intimate Belonging*, by Brennan Manning, Kindle ed., The Navigators, 2015. pp. 44-45.

6. *The Return of the Prodigal Son: A Story of Homecoming*, by Henri J.M. Nouwen, Kindle ed., The Crown Publishing Group, 1994, p. 54.

7. *Life of the Beloved: Spiritual Living in a Secular World with New Guide to Reflection*, by Henri J.M. Nouwen, Kindle ed., The Crossroad Publishing Company, 2002, p. 31.

Chapter Six – The Law of Addiction

1. *Life of the Beloved: Spiritual Living in a Secular World with New Guide to Reflection*, by Henri J.M. Nouwen, Kindle ed., The Crossroad Publishing Company, 2002, p. 31.

2. Ibid, pp. 31-33.

3. "Luke 15:13." *Word Study Greek-English New Testament: a Literal, Interlinear Word Study of the Greek New Testament*; United Bible Societies' Third Corrected Edition with New Revised Standard Version, New Testament, and Word Study Concordance, by Paul R. McReynolds, Tyndale House Publishers, 1999.

4. "A Tale of Two Cities." SparkNotes, 2017, www.sparknotes.com/lit/twocities/themes/.

5. Ibid.

6. Ibid.

7. *The Return of the Prodigal Son: A Story of Homecoming*, by Henri J.M. Nouwen, Kindle ed., The Crown Publishing Group, 1994, p. 54.

8. Hipponensis, Aurelius Augustine, et al. *The City of God*. New City Press, 2018.

9. "Zapping the Zelig." *To Christ I Look: Homilies at Twilight*, by Walter J. Burghardt, Paulist Press, 1989, p. 15.

10. *Abba's Child: The Cry of the Heart for Intimate Belonging*, by Brennan Manning, Kindle ed., The Navigators, 2015, p. 16.

11. Ibid, p. 16.

12. Ibid, p. 17.

13. *Addiction and Grace: Love and Spirituality in the Healing of Addictions*, by Gerald G. May, HarperSanFrancisco, 1988, p. 168.

14. *The Search for the Real Self: Unmasking the Personality Disorders of Our Age*, by James F. Masterson, Free Press, 1988, p. 67.

15. *Encounter with God: A Theology of Christian Experience*, Morton Kelsey quoted by Parker Palmer in "The Monastic Way to Church Renewal," no. 4, Winter, Desert Call, 1987, pp. 8-9.

16. *Merton's Palace of Nowhere: A Search for God Through Awareness of the True Self*, by Thomas Merton quoted by James Finley, Ave Maria Press, 1978, p. 34.

17. *Homecoming: Reclaiming and Championing Your Inner Child*, by John Bradshaw, Bantam Books, 1990, p. 8.

18. *The Return of the Prodigal Son: A Story of Homecoming*, by Henri J.M. Nouwen, Kindle ed., The Crown Publishing Group, 1994, pp. 57-58.

19. Ibid, p. 58.

20. *New Seeds of Contemplation*, by Thomas Merton, New Directions Book, 2007, pp. 8–9.

Chapter Seven – Purgatory: An Affair with Do

1. *The Return of the Prodigal Son: A Story of Homecoming*, by Henri J.M. Nouwen, Kindle ed., The Crown Publishing Group, 1994, p. 57.

2. Carroll, Lewis. "Through the Looking-Glass, And What Alice Found There." *The Project Gutenberg EBook of Through the Looking-Glass*, by Lewis Carroll, 28 April 2021, www.gutenberg.org/files/12/12-h/12-h.htm#link2HCH0002.

3. *The Return of the Prodigal Son: A Story of Homecoming*, by Henri J.M. Nouwen, Kindle ed., The Crown Publishing Group, 1994, p. 56.

4. Ibid, pp. 62-63.

5. *Tale of Two Sons*, by John MacArthur, Kindle ed., Thomas Nelson Publishers, 2008, p. 947.

6. Ibid, p. 1046.

7. Ibid, p. 1166.

8. Ibid, p. 1166.

9. Ibid, p. 1147.

10. *Abba's Child: The Cry of the Heart for Intimate Belonging*, by Brennan Manning, Kindle ed., The Navigators, 2015. p. 25.

11. Subby, Robert, et al. "Inside the Chemically Dependent Marriage: Denial and Manipulation." *Co-Dependency: an Emerging Issue, Health Communications*, 1984, p. 26.

12. *Codependent No More: How to Stop Controlling Others and Start Caring for Yourself*, by Melody Beattie, Kindle ed., Hazelden Publishing, 2016, p. 30.

13. Ibid, pp. 34, 65.

14. *The Search for the Real Self: Unmasking the Personality Disorders of Our Age*, by James F. Masterson, Free Press, 1988, pp. 63, 66.

15. Ibid, pp. 63, 66.

16. *Abba's Child: The Cry of the Heart for Intimate Belonging*, by Brennan Manning, Kindle ed., The Navigators, 2015, p. 22.

17. *The Return of the Prodigal Son: A Story of Homecoming*, Henri J.M. Nouwen, Kindle ed., The Crown Publishing Group, 1994, p. 63.

18. *Shame Interrupted: How God Lifts the Pain of Worthlessness and Rejection*, by Edward T. Welch, New Growth Press, 2012, pp. 11-12.

19. *The Return of the Prodigal Son: A Story of Homecoming*, Henri J.M. Nouwen, Kindle ed., The Crown Publishing Group, 1994, p. 64.

20. Cruz, Antonio. "The Carob Tree." Evangelical Focus, 14 July 2021, evangelicalfocus.com/zoe/3148/the-carob-tree.

21. *The Return of the Prodigal Son: A Story of Homecoming*, by Henri J. M. Nouwen, Kindle Ed., The Crown Publishing Group, 1994, p. 67.

22. *Shame Interrupted: How God Lifts the Pain of Worthlessness and Rejection*, by Edward T. Welch, New Growth Press, 2012, p. 2.

23. *God's passionate Desire and Our Response*, by William Barry, Ave Maria Press, 1993, p. 87. See chapter, "Mysticism in Hell."

24. *Abba's Child: The Cry of the Heart for Intimate Belonging*, by Brennan Manning, Kindle ed., The Navigators, 2015. p. 25.

25. *New Seeds of Contemplation*, by Thomas Merton, New Directions Book, 2007, p. 25.

26. *The Return of the Prodigal Son: A Story of Homecoming*, by Henri J. M. Nouwen, Kindle Ed., The Crown Publishing Group, 1994, pp. 66-67.

Chapter Eight – Change of Heart

1. *An Experience Named Spirit*, by John Shea, Thomas Moore Press, 1983, pp. 115–117. This story, courtesy of Reuben Gold and the Hasidic tradition, was drastically reworked by Shea and used by this author in the way of adaption.

2. *Abba's Child: The Cry of the Heart for Intimate Belonging*, by Manning, Brennan, et al., Kindle ed., The Navigators, 2015, p. 103.

Chapter Nine – Limping Home

1. *The Return of the Prodigal Son: A Story of Homecoming*, by Henri J. M. Nouwen, Kindle ed., The Crown Publishing Group, 1994, p. 69.

2. *A Tale of Two Sons*, by John F. MacArthur, Thomas Nelson, Kindle ed., loc. 1476.

3. *The Return of the Prodigal Son: A Story of Homecoming*, by Henri J.M. Nouwen, Kindle ed., The Crown Publishing Group, 1994, pp. 70-71.

4. *Depression and Other Common Mental Disorders: Global Health Estimate. World Health Organization*, 2017, apps.who.int/iris/bitstream/handle/10665/254610/WHO-MSD-MER-2017.2-eng.pdf.

5. *The Recovery of Love: Christian Mysticism and the Addictive Society*, by Jeffrey D. Imbach, Crossroad, 1992, pp. 62–63.

6. *Shame Interrupted: How God Lifts the Pain of Worthlessness and Rejection*, by Edward T. Welch, New Growth Press, 2012, p. 42.

7. *Abba's Child: The Cry of the Heart for Intimate Belonging*, by Brennan Manning, Kindle ed., The Navigators, 2015, p. 20.

Chapter Ten – Merit is Overrated

1. *A Tale of Two Sons*, by John F. MacArthur, Kindle ed., Thomas Nelson, Kindle ed., loc. 1,519.

2. *You Are the Beloved*, by Henri J. M. Nouwen, Kindle Ed., The Crown Publishing Group, p. 10.

3. *The Soul of Shame: Retelling the Stories We Believe about Ourselves*, by Curt Thompson, IVP Books, 2015, p. 110.

4. Ibid, p. 110.

5. Ibid, p. 110.

6. Ibid, pp. 110-111.

7. Ibid, p. 123.

8. Ibid, p. 123.

9. *Abba's Child: The Cry of the Heart for Intimate Belonging*, by Brennan Manning, Kindle ed., The Navigators, 2015, p. 87.

Chapter Eleven – Grace is Always Greater

1. *Tale of Two Sons*, by John F. MacArthur, Kindle ed., Thomas Nelson Publishers, 2008, loc. 1859.

2. *Life of the Beloved: Spiritual Living in a Secular World with New Guide to Reflection*, by Henri J.M. Nouwen, Kindle ed., The Crossroad Publishing Company, 2002, p. 3.

Chapter Twelve – Getting Over Yourself

1. *True Spirituality*, by Francis Schaeffer, Kindle ed., Tyndale House Publishers, Inc., 2011, p. 3.

2. Ibid, pp. 3-4.

3. Ibid, p. 4.

4. Ibid, p. 4.

5. *Shame Interrupted: How God Lifts the Pain of Worthlessness and Rejection*, by Edward T. Welch, New Growth Press, 2012, p. 92.

6. Ibid, p. 169.

7. *Abba's Child: The Cry of the Heart for Intimate Belonging*, by Brennan Manning, Kindle ed., The Navigators, 2015, p. 52.

8. Ibid, pp. 9-10.

9. *Merton's Palace of Nowhere: a Search for God through Awareness of the True Self*, by James Finley, Ave Maria, 1978, p. 53.

10. Ibid.

11. *Revelations of Divine Love*, by Julián of Norwich and Clifton Wolters, Penguin Books, 1966, ch. 73.

12. *Abba's Child: The Cry of the Heart for Intimate Belonging*, by Brennan Manning et al., Kindle ed., The Navigators, 2015, pp. 11-13.

13. Ibid, pp. 26-27.

14. Ibid, pp. 9-10.

Chapter Thirteen – Life at Home

1. *The Return of the Prodigal Son: A Story of Homecoming*, by Henri J.M. Nouwen, Kindle ed., The Crown Publishing Group, 1994, p. 51.

2. *The Glory of the Church: Studies in Ephesians*, by Homer Austin Kent, BMH Books, 2005, p. 11.

3. *A Greek-English Lexicon of the New Testament and Other Early Christian Literature*, by Frederick W. Danker et al., 3rd ed., University of Chicago Press, 2000, p. 1024.

4. *New Testament Commentary: Exposition of Galatians*, by William Hendriksen, Baker Book House, 1982, p. 82.

5. Hawthorne, Gerald F., et al. "Adoption." *Dictionary of Paul and His Letters A Compendium of Contemporary Biblical Scholarship*, InterVarsity Press, 2015, p. 16.

6. *The Letter to the Ephesians*, by Curtis W. Vaughan, Convention Press, 1963, p. 22.

7. *The Woman Who Was Poor: a Novel*, by Leon Bloy, St. Augustine's Press, 2015.

8. Wenham, Kitty. "Mother Teresa's Sainthood Is a Fraud, Just Like She Was." Medium, 7 September 2016, medium.com/@KittyWenham/mother-teresas-sainthood-is-a-fraud-just-like-she-was-eb395177572.

9. Ibid.

10. Rathi, Pranshu. "Mother Teresa Not a Godly Saint; Skeptics Continue to Cast Doubt over Her Legacy." IBTimes India, 4 September 2016, www.ibtimes.co.in/mother-teresa-not-godly-saint-skeptics-continue-cast-doubt-over-her-legacy-692402.

11. *Abba's Child: The Cry of the Heart for Intimate Belonging*, by Brennan Manning, Kindle ed., The Navigators, 2015, p. 32.

12. *Drawn into the Mystery of God through the Gospel of John*, by Jean Vanier, Paulist Press, 2004, p. 296.

Chapter Fourteen – Tailor-Made

1. *Shame Interrupted: How God Lifts the Pain of Worthlessness and Rejection*, by Edward T. Welch, New Growth Press, 2012, p. 78.

2. Ibid, p. 78.

3. Ibid, pp. 65-66.

4. Ibid, p. 75.

5. *The Pentateuch*, by L. Thomas Holdcroft, CeeTeC Publishing, 1996, p. 167.

6. *Shame Interrupted: How God Lifts the Pain of Worthlessness and Rejection*, by Edward T. Welch, New Growth Press, 2012, p. 79.

7. Ibid, p. 82.

Chapter Fifteen – The Art of Celebration

1. *The Wedding Party*, by Timothy Keller, Encounters with Jesus Series Book 4, Viking, 2013.

2. Ibid.

3. *Encounters With Jesus*, by Timothy Keller, Kindle ed., Penguin Books, 2016, p. 107.

4. Ibid.

5. *The Sermon of Jonathan Edwards*, by W. Kimnach, K. Minkema, D. Sweeney, Des, 1999, pp. 127-128.

6. *The Brothers Karamazov*, by Fyodor Dostoyevsky, Kindle ed., Pandora's Box, 2020, p. 370.

7. Spurgeon, Charles H. "Many Kisses for Returning Sinners, or Prodigal Love for the Prodigal Son (March 29th, 1891)." Prodigal Love for the Prodigal Son, Midwestern Baptist Theological Seminary, archive.spurgeon.org/sermons/2236.php.

8. *The Prodigal God*, by Timothy Keller, Kindle ed., Penguin Publishing Group, pp. 105-106.

Chapter Sixteen – Doers are Party Poopers

1. *A Tale of Two Sons*, by John F. MacArthur, Kindle ed., Thomas Nelson, loc. 2239.

2. Ibid, loc. 2272.

3. Ibid, loc. 2283.

4. *A Tale of Two Sons*, by John F. MacArthur, Kindle ed., Thomas Nelson, loc. 2325.

5. Ibid, loc. 2378.

6. Ibid, loc. 2378.

Chapter Seventeen – The Initiative is with Who?

1. *Abba's Child: The Cry of the Heart for Intimate Belonging*, by Brennan Manning, Kindle ed., The Navigators, 2015, p. 3.

2. Ibid, p. 3.

3. Ibid, p. 65.

4. *Soul Making: The Desert Way of Spirituality*, by Alan Jones, HarperCollins, 1989, p. 37.

5. *Abba's Child: The Cry of the Heart for Intimate Belonging*, by Brennan Manning, Kindle ed., The Navigators, 2015, p. 59.

6. *Why I Am Not A Christian: And other essays on religion and related subjects*, by Russell Bertrand, Simon & Schuster, 1957, p. 35.

7. *Abba's Child: The Cry of the Heart for Intimate Belonging*, by Brennan Manning, Kindle ed., The Navigators, 2015, p. 63.

8. Ibid, p. 65.

9. Ibid, pp. 64-65.

10. *The Furious Longing of God*, by Brennan Manning, Kindle ed., David C Cook, pp. 124-128.

11. *The Furious Longing of God*, by Brennan Manning, Kindle Edition, David C Cook, pp. 124-128. Excerpt is used by permission by David C Cook.

12. *Holman New Testament Commentary: Luke*, by Max Anders, ed., Trent C. Butler author, B&H Publishing Group, 2000, p. 174.

13. Ibid.

Chapter Eighteen – To be or Not to Be

1. *The Cross and the Prodigal: Luke 15 Through the Eyes of Middle Eastern Peasants*, by Kenneth E. Bailey, Revised ed., IVP Books, 2005.

2. *Abba's Child: The Cry of the Heart for Intimate Belonging*, by Brennan Manning et al., Kindle ed., The Navigators, 2015, p. 74.

3. Ibid, p. 95.

4. Ibid, p. 91.

5. Ibid, pp. 41-42.

6. *You Are the Beloved*, by Henri J. M. Nouwen, Kindle ed., The Crown Publishing Group, 2017, p. 16.

7. *Life of the Beloved: Spiritual Living in a Secular World*, by Henri J. M. Nouwen, Crossroad, 1992, p. 26.

8. Ibid.

9. *The Spiritual Exercises of St. Ignatius: A Literal Translation and a Contemporary Reading*, by David L. Fleming, The Institute of Jesuit Sources, 1978, p. 115.

10. Ibid.

11. *Holman New Testament Commentary: Luke*, by Max Anders, ed., Trent C. Butler author, B&H Publishing Group, 2000, p. 221.

Chapter Nineteen – The Ordinary Christian Life

1. *With Open Hands*, by Henri J. M. Nouwen, Kindle ed., Ave Maria Press, 2006, p. 20.

2. Ibid, pp. 20-21.

3. Ibid, p. 20.

4. Ibid, p. 23.

5. Ibid, pp. 25-26.

Chapter Twenty – Made Alive

1. *Shame Interrupted: How God Lifts the Pain of Worthlessness and Rejection*, by Edward T. Welch, New Growth Press, 2012, p. 103.

2. Ibid.

3. *True Spirituality*, by Francis Schaeffer, Crossway Books, 2020, p. 200.

Chapter Twenty-One – Engaging the Monotony with Celebration

1. *THE EPISTLES OF OVID (ENGLISH)*, by P. Ovidius Naso, Perseus Digital Library, Ovid Epistulae, 4.103.141.

2. James S. Jeffers, *The Greco-Roman World of the New Testament Era: Exploring the Background of Early Christianity*, InterVarsity Press, Downers Grove, IL, 1999, p. 21.

3. *Jerusalem in the Time of Jesus: An Investigation into Economic and Social Conditions during the New Testament Period*, by Joachim Jeremais. F.H. and C.H. Cave translators, 3rd ed., Fortress Press, pp. 310-11.

4. Ibid, p. 310.

5. Ibid, pp. 310-311.

6. Ibid, p. 310.

7. Ibid, p. 312.

Chapter Twenty-Two – If There's Anything to Do, Then Sit

1. *True Spirituality*, by Francis Schaeffer, Kindle ed., Tyndale House Publishers, Inc., 2011, p. 5.

2. *Sit, Walk, Stand: The Process of Christian Maturity*, by Watchman Nee, Kindle ed., CLC Publications, 1977, p. 9.

3. Ibid, p. 10.

4. Ibid, p. 10.

5. *If It's Not Broken, Break it!*, by George Morrison, Viacom Inc., 1992, p. 51.

6. *The Normal Christian Life*, by Watchman Nee, Kindle ed., Living Stream Ministry, 1993, p. 32.

7. Ibid, p. 32.

8. Ibid, pp. 32-33.

www.ingramcontent.com/pod-product-compliance
Lightning Source LLC
Chambersburg PA
CBHW011233160426
43209CB00042B/1986/J